The New York Times

PUBLIC PROFILES

Ruth Bader Ginsburg

THE NEW YORK TIMES EDITORIAL STAFF

Published in 2020 by New York Times Educational Publishing
in association with The Rosen Publishing Group, Inc.
29 East 21st Street, New York, NY 10010

First Edition

The New York Times
Alex Ward: Editorial Director, Book Development
Phyllis Collazo: Photo Rights/Permissions Editor
Heidi Giovine: Administrative Manager

Rosen Publishing
Megan Kellerman: Managing Editor
Wendy Wong: Editor
Greg Tucker: Creative Director
Brian Garvey: Art Director

Cataloging-in-Publication Data
Names: New York Times Company.
Title: Ruth Bader Ginsburg / edited by the New York Times
editorial staff.
Description: New York : New York Times Educational Publishing,
2020. | Series: Public profiles | Includes glossary and index.
Identifiers: ISBN 9781642822458 (library bound) | ISBN
9781642822441 (pbk.) | ISBN 9781642822465 (ebook)
Subjects: LCSH: Ginsburg, Ruth Bader—Juvenile literature. |
United States. Supreme Court—Biography—Juvenile literature. |
Judges—United States—Biography—Juvenile literature. | Women
judges—United States—Biography—Juvenile literature.
Classification: LCC KF8745.G56 R884 2020 |
DDC 347.73'2634 B—dc23

Manufactured in the United States of America

On the cover: Supreme Court Justice Ruth Bader Ginsburg poses
for the court's official portrait in Washington, D.C., Nov. 30, 2018;
Chip Somodevilla/Getty Images.

Contents

CHAPTER 3

Supreme Court Decisions

CHAPTER 4

Speaking Up and Speaking Out

CHAPTER 5

In Sickness and in Health

CHAPTER 6

Screen, Stage and Pages

Introduction

WHEN RUTH BADER GINSBURG attended Harvard Law School, she was one of nine women in her year. One evening during dinner, the dean asked each female student why she was there, taking a spot that could've gone to a man.

Ginsburg has spent her life putting her education and passion for the legal system to good use despite those who continue to ask that same question. She graduated with top honors from Columbia Law School. She was a professor at Rutgers University, where she taught courses on women and the law, before becoming the first woman to teach full-time at Columbia Law School. She co-founded the Women's Rights Project, a sector of the American Civil Liberties Union. She argued and won gender discrimination cases before the Supreme Court. She served as a federal appeals court judge for Washington, D.C., before taking her place as a Supreme Court justice.

Ginsburg's reserved demeanor masked her fierce resilience and refusal to accept that a woman's place was merely as the law described it. She persistently highlighted areas of gender inequality in the law and the ways they hindered both women and men, working to put the sexes on equal footing in all areas of life from the workforce to the home. With each court case she won and law she overturned, she sought to open the eyes of lawmakers and to benefit society with more progressive ideas and values.

Her family is incredibly important to her, serving as the foundation for her accomplishments. Her husband, Marty, and her two children, Jane and James, consistently encouraged her persistence and work ethic. When Ginsburg was a child, her mother, Celia, was a strong role model who disciplined her and taught her the importance of a good

Ruth Bader Ginsburg in 1972, when she was named a professor at Columbia Law School.

education. She was taught to be independent, to think about her decisions and live for herself, not for someone else. She did not believe the sole purpose of her life was to be a wife, mother or caregiver. Her mother also imparted valuable advice, teaching her that words and actions fueled by anger and resentment would only result in a losing battle. Ginsburg took that message to heart, making sure to remain courteous and composed regardless of the unfair comments and treatment she would receive. She wholeheartedly respected the law even as she worked to change it. Although she often disagreed with other Supreme Court justices, she didn't allow any personal feelings to escalate and leave the courtroom. She surrounded herself with people who stood at opposing sides of various issues, forging strong ties with her fellow justices, politicians and social activists.

In addition to being a well-respected name in legal and political circles, Ginsburg has become a buzz-worthy pop culture phenomenon. As a result of her much-deserved level of celebrity, she's been introduced to younger generations who've been inspired to learn about who she is and all the things she has done — and continues to do — to champion equal rights for all. She's been on both sides of the judge's bench, playing crucial roles in important cases that have been the foundation of women's rights and the dismantling of gender discrimination. Even now, she continues to work and push past obstacles like her numerous health problems and calls for her resignation, remaining as focused and passionate as when she first began.

CHAPTER 1

Rising Through the Ranks

As a Harvard Law School student, Ruth Bader Ginsburg became an expert at juggling her schoolwork while taking care of her newborn daughter, Jane, and her husband, Marty, who was diagnosed with testicular cancer. She transferred to Columbia Law School and graduated at the top of her class, only to be rejected by numerous law firms in New York City because of her sex. Her experiences in school, as both professor and appellate court judge, strengthened her fearless approach in confronting gender discrimination, inspiring many in her uphill climb toward what would become the defining role of her career.

Columbia Law Snares a Prize in the Quest for Women Professors

BY LESLEY OELSNER | **JAN. 26, 1972**

IN A NEW ACCELERATING competition among the nation's law schools, Columbia University has just scored a major coup: its law school, to its undisguised glee, has just bid for and won a woman for the job of full professor — the first in its 114-year history.

The glee comes in part because the woman, Ruth Bader Ginsburg, is what the school's dean, Michael Sovern, calls "so distinguished a scholar," that her credentials and honors would stand out in any catalogue of professors.

It comes too, as the University of Michigan Law School dean, Theodore St. Antoine, says, at a time when many of the country's best law schools have been "scrambling" for women, often for the same one. Most have no women at any rung of the professorial ladder, and, according to other sources, the woman Columbia got was among those being scrambled for.

And the glee is likely to spread far beyond the Columbia law faculty and into the law schools, where women students have long sensed an anti-female bias.

The appointment of Mrs. Ginsburg does not add to the handful of women now working as full professors of law, for she has been a full professor at Rutgers, the State University of New Jersey, since 1969. It does, however, mark the first time that Columbia Law has chosen a woman for a full-time post higher than lecturer, or part-time post higher than adjunct professor.

SEVERAL WOMEN CHOSEN

Beyond that, it coincides with the selection this winter of women by a few equally well-regarded schools, including Stanford, the University of California at Los Angeles and Yale, as assistant or associate professors. All the appointments are, as in Mrs. Ginsburg's case, subject to approval by the governing boards of the respective universities and effective next fall.

The deans say that the search for women, begun a couple of years ago but intensified considerably since then, is now under way from Harvard to Indiana University to Stanford. A major reason for this new effort, the deans said in interviews, is the increased number of women now coming out of law school, now about 10 per cent of the graduates and growing. The lack of available women in the past, they said, was the reason for the present paucity of female faculty members.

But there were other reasons offered for the present effort too, ranging from the demand by the increasing number of female law students for female professors to an appreciation of the benefits of a diversified faculty, to the "realization," in Mr. St. Antoine's words, that "law is a profession that a woman can handle as well as a man" — or, as Murray Schwartz of U.C.L.A. put it, to the fact that "whatever bias or prejudice or whatever you'd call it by the male faculty against hiring women" has disappeared.

PHILOSOPHICAL ATTITUDES

Professor Ginsburg, for her part, takes a philosophical stance — pleased with some of the progress to date and delighted to be going to Columbia, but anything but pollyanish as to prospects for future change.

In an interview she recalled that when she graduated from Columbia Law she was tied for first place in her class.

But she could not get a job with a law firm, she said. At first, when the rejection notices started coming in, she thought something might be wrong with her, but then, she said, "when I got so many rejections, I thought it couldn't be they had no use for me — it had to be something else."

So she got, upon graduation, a job clerking for a Federal district judge — whereas, as anyone familiar with the subject knows, and as she refrained from pointing out, a man with those grades from that school could have gotten a clerkship in a Federal appeals court, if not the United States Supreme Court.

Later she went to Rutgers, where, for her first few years, she feels, there was some discrimination. That stopped after a while, she said, but last fall, as a visiting professor at Harvard Law, giving a course involving women's rights, she noticed a little of the same male wariness there too.

"The law teachers are like that mostly," she said, feeling that the women's movement "threatens a way of life they find very comfortable."

What does she expect, and how will she act, she was asked, when she goes to Columbia this fall, to teach procedure, conflicts and a special course, in conjunction with the American Civil Liberties Union, on sex discrimination?

Said Professor Ginsburg, the 38-year-old wife of a successful tax lawyer and mother of a girl, 16, and a boy, 6: "The only confining thing for me is time. I'm not going to curtail my activities in any way to please them."

"I don't think I'll have any problem," she added a moment later. "People will be pleasant on the outside. Some of them may have reservations about what I'm doing, but I don't think they'll be expressed."

At any rate, her new role is far from what was expected of her in her girlhood, when, she recalled: "No one ever expected me to go to law school. I was supposed to be a high school teacher, or how else could I earn a living?"

A Widower Sues for Benefits

BY RICHARD J. H. JOHNSTON | MARCH 11, 1973

EDISON, N. J. — A woman lawyer from New York and the Women's Rights Project of the American Civil Liberties Union in Newark have joined forces in an attempt to obtain Social Security benefits for a widowed father.

On behalf of Stephen C. Wiesenfeld, a 29-year-old mathematician and computer expert, and "all other persons similarly situated," a suit has been filed in United States District Court in Newark. It asks that the payment of "mother's insurance benefits" to widows be extended to fathers whose wives have died and left them with a child or children. The only benefits now available to widowers start at age 62.

Mr. Wiesenfeld's wife, Paula, died in childbirth last June 5, leaving her husband with a son, Jason Paul. Mrs. Wiesenfeld, a graduate of the University of Michigan, was a teacher in the high school here when she died.

In the seven years before her death, Mr. Wiesenfeld said, his wife had paid maximum Social Security premiums while teaching in White Plains, N. Y., and Edison.

After her death, Mr. Wiesenfeld applied at the Social Security office in New Brunswick for benefits to which he and his son might be entitled under the Social Security laws.

"I was told," he said, "that my son was eligible for child insurance benefits, but that benefits for the surviving male parent, although he was caring for his child in an identical situation as a widow would be, were payable only to women and not to men."

Since that visit, Mr. Wiesenfeld has been receiving child insurance payments for his son, they average about $248 a month. Had Mr. Wiesenfeld died and his wife survived, she would be receiving from Social Security payments equal to about the same amount as that received for the child.

Mr. Wiesenfeld's lawyers are headed by Ruth Bader Ginsburg, a professor at Columbia University Law School and a practicing attorney in New York State. They contend that he is being denied the payments solely on the ground of his sex.

In the complaint filed in District Court, it is argued by Mr. Wiesenfeld that "on the sole ground that he is a father — not a mother, a widower [or] a widow," he is denied due process and equal protection guaranteed by the Fifth Amendment to the Constitution.

Mr. Wiesenfeld said that he had found Social Security officials on the local level sympathetic, but that they felt forced to stand firmly on the reading of the existing law. It refers in such cases only to "mother's insurance benefits." The suit names the Secretary of Health, Education and Welfare as the responsible defendant for the administration and enforcement of the Social Security Act.

Mr. Wiesenfeld, a native of the Bronx, was graduated from Taft High School in 1961. He is employed by "Cyphernetics," a computer counseling service in Springfield.

The young father has turned aside all offers from members of his family and from friends to take over the care of Jason Paul.

"I intend to raise my son," he said. "I want to be a father to him. I realize I cannot be a mother, but I don't want the tie between us broken."

Meanwhile, Mr. Wiesenfeld employs a housekeeper by day and, infrequently, a sitter for the evenings. He intends to keep his 10-room house here. Visits from his parents on occasional weekends give him a degree of freedom, he says.

Mr. Wiesenfeld hurries home from his office at about 5:30 P.M., takes charge of feeding his son and puts him to bed. In the morning, they have breakfast together.

Mr. Wiesenfeld said there were no late-night feedings and that he and Jason Paul appeared to have arrived at a gentleman's agreement about uninterrupted sleep.

"And," he said, "we seem to like the same fruit juice and cereal."

3-Piece Suits, Not Women, Scarce at a Law Parley

BY LESLEY OELSNER | MARCH 23, 1975

STANFORD, CALIF., MARCH 22 — One thousand law students, scores of lawyers, a large assortment of professors and officials and at least one judge have come here from across the country for a conference on the law. It is not, however, at all like the usual conventions of lawyers.

No one is wearing a threepiece suit, or even a pin stripe.

The registration room has one table offering "child care" and another offering "alternative housing."

A judge and the judge's associates were mistaken by waitresses at their hotel for a convention of secretaries.

And, almost everyone is female.

It is the sixth National Conference on Woman and Law, co-sponsored this year by the Women of Stanford Law and the California Commission on the Status of Women.

MOSTLY, IT IS A WORKING MEETING, with a schedule of 75 workshops. Half of them are "overviews," giving a picture of the legal developments involving women in such areas as employment discrimination, health care, tax and criminal law. The rest are "technicals," with specific advice and information on, among other things, litigation strategies, affirmative action programs and divorce law.

At 9 this morning, the first 15 workshops began.

In Room 380X of the Mathematics Building at Stanford University, Prof. Ruth Bader Ginsburg of Columbia Law School and Nancy Duff Campbell, assistant professor at Catholic University Law School, started their workshop on women and welfare.

Professor Ginsburg has argued most of the major sex discrimination cases before the Supreme Court in the last few years, including the Wiesenfeld case involving Social Security benefits decided in her favor by the court this week. She was also the keynote speaker at the conference last night, getting two standing ovations. This morning, Room 380X was packed — with students, a judge, and a large contingent of lawyers.

"The Social Security system discriminates against women," she said, and proceeded to list the ways — by exacting a higher contribution without a correspondingly higher benefit for two-earner families, for instance; by not insuring a homemaker in her own right; by failing to take into account the fact that many women workers will take a period off from full-time work, but only temporarily, while their children are small.

Down the hall, in Room 380C, several dozen other lawyers and law students were hearing of employment discrimination. In 380Y, the subject was criminal law.

THE CONFERENCE IS the latest in a series that began in 1969 at New York University Law School, with a small meeting of about 100 people, almost all law students, convened to provide a way for women law students in various schools to communicate with one another and improve their prospects in the legal profession.

This year 650 people, lawyers as well as law students, pre-registered for the conference. Several hundred more are expected by the conference's close tomorrow afternoon, and well over 100 lawyers and professors are directing the panels.

The total budget is $55,000 to be covered, the conference planners hope, by registration fees and contributions and a group of grants from foundations — including $500 from the Playboy Foundation.

Officially, there are now three main purposes for the meeting — to educate law students about women's rights, to enable lawyers involved in litigation about women's rights in various parts of the country to trade information, and to install some interest about women's rights in lawyers not yet involved in the area.

There appear to be some other purposes as well.

"I'm the only one," says Kamilla Mazanec of her status as the sole female professor at Chase Law School in Covington, Ky. "Every place I've been, I've been the only one, the first and only. It gets very lonely sometimes."

MEN ARE NOT BANNED from attending — indeed one of the workshop leaders is male, Prof. Leo Kanowitz of the Hastings College of Law, and several dozen men have registered as participants.

There is, however, a certain amount of role-reversal going on.

Some of Stanford Law School's male students have been helping out at the conference, but, as Marsha Greenfield, the conference administrator, says, "not for major jobs." The men have been called on, she says, "when we need hands to stuff envelopes," or to do other menial tasks.

Some of the men who registered, moreover, are here as husbands — men like John Corwin, a 27-year-old lawyer, with the Legal Aid Society in New York City. His wife, Laurie Woods, a lawyer with Mobilization for Youth in New York, registered months ago, and Mr. Corwin decided at the last moment to come along as well.

One of the few men who appeared to come to the conference alone is Charley McNabb, a student at the law school at the University of Houston. He got interested in women's rights originally, he says, when he realized that while women made up only 30 per cent of the student body, they made up "more than half of the first 10 per cent" in academic standing.

"When I get out," he says, "I want to practice with the best lawyers available."

Law Parley Finds Women Lagging in Rights

BY LESLEY OELSNER | MARCH 27, 1975

PALO ALTO, CALIF., MARCH 4 — Courts and legislatures have dramatically changed the legal status of women in recent years, bringing it far closer to that of men. But a substantial gap remains, with women around the country sometimes denied rights that men have, other times given different rights.

A thousand lawyers and law students, nearly all of them women, reviewed the progress to date and the problems remaining during the National Conference on Women and the Law here this weekend. They found both gains and gaps in areas as diverse as employment and taxation, in situations ranging from that of women as parents and women as victims of crime.

Ruth Bader Ginsburg, the Columbia Law School professor who has argued most of the recent major sex discrimination cases before the Supreme Court, put it this way:

"Realizing the equality principle will require a long and persistent effort, after the artificial barriers are removed, to prevent perpetuation of the effects of past discrimination long into the future."

Among the major areas covered were the following:

THE SOCIAL SECURITY SYSTEM

Last week the Supreme Court handed the women's movement one of its most significant court victories to date; a unanimous ruling that the Social Security law's system of denying child care benefits to the spouse of a deceased female wage earner, while providing those benefits to the spouse of a deceased male wage earner, was unconstitutional.

Most of the Supreme Court Justices, according to Professor Ginsburg, who argued the case, appeared to base their decision largely on the fact that the law denigrated the work of women — providing less protection for the families of women wage earners than for the families of men wage earners.

The Social Security law has other features, however, which also treat women workers differently from men workers.

One of those, in the view of women's rights proponents, is the Social Security System's failure to provide any independent coverage for women who work in the home, as housewives, as opposed to in the market place.

Another is the effect of provisions covering two-earner families, with both husband and wife contributing through Social Security payments during their working lives.

A husband and wife "who work through their lives might have less money on retirement than a one earner family with the same income" as a result of those provisions, Margaret Gates, director of the center for women's policy studies in Washington told participants at the conference.

Still another feature of the Social Security System provides that people who leave the work force for five years are not entitled to receive disability benefits until they have re-entered the work force and worked another five years. Said Professor Ginsburg, this "ignores the fact" that most women have intervals in their working careers when they drop out of full-time work in order to bear and rear children.

The Advisory Council on Social Security, appointed last year and required to report regularly on the system to both Congress and the President, has recommended removing some but not all of the features that critics consider discriminatory.

TAXATION

According to Susan Spivack, a visiting professor at Stanford and a panelist at the conference here, several aspects of the tax system "operate to make it disadvantageous for the secondary wage earner to work" — and the secondary wage earner, the one who earns less than the wage earner in the family, is most often the wife.

Among other things, there are strict limitations on deductions for the costs of child care incurred when a mother goes to work outside the home, and the progressive tax rate, when combined with the system of aggregating the incomes of the husband and wife, can also work to create what Professor Spivak called a "disincentive" to women would-be workers.

THE JURY SYSTEM

Women are now entitled to serve on juries in Federal as well as state courts. This is a relatively new right, in that a few states continued to exclude women from their courts' juries even into the nineteen-sixties, and that until 1957, the right to serve on a jury in a Federal District Court depended on the law of the state in which the court sat.

Last January, the Supreme Court, in the case of Taylor v. Louisiana, struck down Louisiana's system of requiring women, but not men, to "affirmatively register" if they wanted to serve as jurors. The Court said that exempting women from jury service solely because of their sex violated a defendant's right under the Sixth Amendment to have a jury drawn from a cross-section of the community.

However, according to one of the panelists at the conference — Liz Schneider of the Center for Constitutional Rights in New York — the Taylor case may not have as broad an effect as women's rights advocates would like.

The facts in the Taylor case were particularly strong, she said, with no women at all in the jury pool used in the case involved in the court's decisions; it is thus possible that the decision will not be applied in cases where at least some women are in the pool.

Even if all affirmative registration systems are struck down, moreover, according to Rhonda Copelon, another lawyer at the center, other discriminatory features of the jury system remain. Among them: laws in four states that grant an absolute exemption to women, which they can claim if they wish; exemptions in many Federal courts and some state courts for women with children, regardless of whether or not the woman actually needs to be at home to take care of the children.

EMPLOYMENT

Title VII of the Civil Rights Act prohibits discrimination based on sex in employment opportunity covered by the act and a number of suits have been brought and either won or successfully settled under the act, often with affirmative action programs. But the recession is threatening some of those gains — particularly through the so-called "LIFO" system, or "last in first out," provided for in some labor contracts.

PREGNANCY

The law relating to pregnancy has likewise seen some changes, but nowhere near as many as women's rights leaders would like.

The Supreme Court's rulings invalidating anti-abortion laws were one major gain. Another was the Court's invalidation of a required maternity leave at four months of pregnancy for public school teachers in Cleveland.

However, the Court in another case refused to strike down a provision of California's disability insurance system that denied payments for disabilities of normal pregnancies.

A similar pattern is seen in other areas as well. Marilyn G. Haft, director of the American Civil Liberties Union's sexual privacy project, noted during the conference that the courts in a few states have found that prostitution laws are unconstitutional to the extent that they provide only for the prosecution of women prostitutes, not of male prostitutes or customers of prostitutes.

Judge Lisa Richette of the Court of Common Pleas in Philadelphia, noted that some jurisdictions are easing the burden of proof required in rape cases, a burden that has traditionally been higher than in other types of cases.

EQUAL RIGHTS AMENDMENT

The rights amendment, if passed, is expected to do much to change this pattern of scattered gains and lingering discrimination. As for the reasons underlying the pattern, lawyers suggest that at least some of the gains to date have come because the various laws involved have been so blatantly discriminatory — "easy cases," in lawyers' terminology.

Professor Ginsburg suggested an additional reason: There is a certain ambivalence in the society, she said, and courts, including the Supreme Court, reflect it:

"Conditions of contemporary life demand recognition that distinct roles for men and women coerced or steered by law are antithetical to the American ideal of freedom of choice for the individual. But action based on that recognition is deterred by fear — fear of unsettling familiar and, for many men and women, comfortable patterns."

The Legal Profession Is Absorbing an Influx of Women

SPECIAL TO THE NEW YORK TIMES | APRIL 18, 1978

CAMBRIDGE, MASS., APRIL 16 — In the late 1950's, when Prof. Ruth Bader Ginsburg was a student at Harvard Law School, "women were not looked upon as people who should be there," she recalled. Prosecutors' offices would not assign women to criminal cases, only a handful of women taught law and the pace-setting law firms wanted no women at all.

When Professor Ginsburg, who teaches at Columbia University Law School, entered in 1956, there were 30 women enrolled at Harvard Law School. Now there are 394.

Across the country, as law school enrollments have climbed, probably the greatest change in the last decade has been the influx of women. Of the country's 118,453 law students, 32,934 are women. That is 10 times the number of women enrolled 10 years ago and nearly as many as the total number of law students 25 years ago.

CHANGE 'FOR THE BETTER'

"What is happening is that the legal profession is being transformed, and for the better." Albert M. Sacks, Dean of Harvard Law School, told 300 female law students and graduates this weekend. They gathered here to mark the 25th anniversary of Harvard Law's first graduating class to include women.

Of the country's 460,000 practicing lawyers, from 35,000 to 40,000 are women, and, in contrast to the days when Professor Ginsburg was a student, women are now routinely prosecuting, counseling and teaching.

Still, there are areas where gains can still be made:

• At Harvard, the country's largest law school, only one woman is professor, and slightly less than quarter of its students are women, which is fewer than most other law schools have.

• By and large women who are lawyers have yet to crack the bastions of white male conservatism: partnerships in Wall Street and Park Avenue firms in New York City and in large corporate firms elsewhere.

• Some law graduates still complain that they are not treated on an equal footing with men, either in law school or afterward, although most acknowledge that the days of blatant discrimination are past.

"For those of you who are still students," wrote a 1977 graduate, "contrary to popular belief and Harvard propaganda, life is better, and one hell of a lot less sexist, outside those ivy walls than inside."

She was writing anonymously for a directory of the 1,000 women who have graduated from the Harvard Law School in the last quarter-century. But her view is not necessarily the prevailing one.

Many graduates said law practice was worse than school; others said both were unpleasant and still others looked back fondly on law school.

"I loved it here," said Sheila A. Kuehl, a 37-year-old third-year student at Harvard who helped organize this weekend's "Celebration 25."

COURTROOM EXPERIENCE COMMON

Miss Kuehl picked a smaller firm to join in the fall in the hope of gaining greater exposure to courtroom work.

Until the last few years, courtroom doors were virtually shut to women, no matter where they worked. The few women who did graduate from law school went into government work, became law librarians or were relegated to such fields as trusts and estates work, where contact with clients was limited.

At that time, the large firms in New York and around the nation resembled exclusive men's clubs, with partners who were white, male and Protestant. In the last few years, however, scores of women and a handful of members of minorities have joined major New York law firms as associates, with starting salaries of at least $25,000.

In part, the firms changed their minds about women only after some of them had been sued on the ground of discrimination and they had been forced to agree to offer significantly more jobs to women. The firms have also begun to hire women because failure to do so would have deprived them of many of the best young legal minds. And, in part, the hiring of women reflects a greater acceptance of working women.

In panel discussions at Harvard over the weekend, women said that they now perceived little difference between the working conditions for them and men in large firms. They said that they had been given caseloads equal to those given men as well as responsibilities commensurate with their experience.

Even so, women have not reached the most responsible positions in New York firms, which still are the big drawing cards for male and female graduates of the top law schools, or in most prominent firms elsewhere. Of 750 or so partners in New York City's 20 largest firms, fewer than two dozen are women.

But, as Dean Sacks of Harvard pointed out in an interview, relatively few women have reached the point, six, seven or eight years out of law school, where partnership is considered.

"It will have to come," he said. "The pressure is hydraulic."

And women have been gaining a foothold in other law careers that have traditionally been male preserves. In the Manhattan District Attorney's office, 56 of the 229 prosecutors are women, as against 14 of the 165 lawyers five years ago.

In Hackensack, N.J., Sybil R. Moses has been prosecuting the seven-week-old curare murder trial of Dr. Mario E. Jascalevich.

Two years ago, when Robert Fiske was named head of the United States Attorney's office in Manhattan, six of the 100 lawyers were women. Now there are 18.

"I hire absolutely on merit," said Mr. Fiske, who has no hesitation in assigning women to prosecute the most complex criminal cases. Women "are particularly effective in litigation," he said, and "they are particularly effective with juries."

Columbia Professor
Studied for Federal Court Post

SPECIAL TO THE NEW YORK TIMES | DEC. 16, 1979

WASHINGTON, DEC. 15 — The Carter Administration has taken a preliminary step toward nominating Ruth Bader Ginsburg, a professor at Columbia Law School and a leading advocate of women's rights, for a seat on the United States Court of Appeals for the District of Columbia.

According to legal sources here, the name of Professor Ginsburg, 46 years old, has been sent for background checks to the American Bar Association and the Federal Bureau of Investigation.

Professor Ginsburg has drafted many arguments used in major constitutional law cases involving allegations of sex discrimination and is a recognized authority in the fields of constitutional law and civil procedure.

She is a graduate of Cornell University and Columbia Law School. She taught at the Rutgers Law School in Newark from 1963 to 1972 and joined the Columbia law faculty in 1972.

When asked to comment on the report, Professor Ginsburg said that she knew her name had been on the list of nine candidates submitted in March by the District of Columbia's judicial nominating commission but added that it would be inappropriate for her to discuss the possible appointment.

Should her nomination be approved by the Senate, Professor Ginsburg would take the seat on the appeals court that had been held since 1965 by Judge Harold Leventhal, who died as a result of a heart attack last month.

Professor Ginsburg's husband, Martin, is also a professor at Columbia Law School, where he was recently named to the newly created Charles Keller Beekman professorship.

Day Cites Law Role of Women

BY DAVID MARGOLICK | APRIL 14, 1984

IN 1873, WHEN THE United States Supreme Court ruled that Myra Bradwell was not Constitutionally entitled to practice law, Justice Joseph B. Bradley wrote what was to become for feminists a landmark opinion.

"The natural and proper timidity and delicacy which belongs to the female sex evidently unfits it for many of the occupations of civil life," Justice Bradley stated. "The paramount destiny and mission of woman are to fulfill the noble and benign office of wife and mother. This is the law of the Creator."

Yesterday was the fifth annual Myra Bradwell Day at Columbia Law School, where nearly one-third of the student body and 10 faculty members are women. Apparently, Representative Geraldine A. Ferraro of Queens reflected in her keynote address, Bradwell v. Illinois was no longer good law.

"If we were ever timid or delicate, we aren't any more," she told 150 students, professors and alumni at the school. "We are fitted for all the occupations of life, with the possible exception of fatherhood."

PORTRAIT IS UNVEILED

The speech by Mrs. Ferraro was the highlight of the Bradwell Day program, named for an Illinois resident who, despite the adverse ruling in 1873, eventually became one of the first women licensed to argue before the Supreme Court.

The day, organized by the Columbia Law Women's Association, ended with the unveiling of a portrait of Judge Ruth Bader Ginsburg of the Federal Court of Appeals in Washington, a former student and faculty member at Columbia.

Judge Ginsburg's portrait, to hang with those of former Chief Justices Charles Evans Hughes and Harlan F. Stone, is the 37th portrait at the Law School. The first 36 are of men.

Representative Geraldine A. Ferraro.

Like most leading American law schools, Columbia was at first reluctant to admit women. In 1890, a trustee of the school declared that "no woman shall degrade herself by practicing law in New York if I can save her" and predicted that "the clack of these possible Portias" would never be admitted here.

The school's opposition to admitting women, it turns out, stemmed not from questions of competence but fears that the women would scare men into going to the Harvard Law School instead.

It was only in 1928 that the school accepted its first woman.

In recent years, however, the face of the school has changed dramatically. Thus, yesterday's events, while designed to air issues of concern to women in the bar, had a ring of celebration.

"I think the women at Columbia are just as happy, or unhappy, as their male counterparts," said Jessica Pincus of the women's association. "I don't think many of us feel terribly discriminated against and I think the opportunities now are almost limitless."

Mrs. Ferraro, who received no job offers upon graduating from Fordham Law School in 1960, devoted most of her speech to politics, charging that the Reagan Administration's cuts in food stamps, housing, legal services and welfare had affected women disproportionately. President Reagan's re-election, she said, would be "a disaster" for women.

"The day seems nearer than I once thought for our nation to have its first woman President or Vice President," she said. "But we are now at a stage when we must work on the second and third and the hundredth woman — to move beyond tokenism to power."

Judge Ginsburg, a 1959 graduate of the law school, became in 1972 the first woman to receive tenure as a faculty member. Before her appointment to the bench in 1980 by President Carter, she earned a reputation as a vigorous advocate for women's rights.

The law school's dean, Albert J. Rosenthal, acknowledged her work at yesterday's ceremony. "Nobody has played as large a role in the elimination in gender discrimination as Ruth did," he said.

Judge Ginsburg, the mother of two, warned in her remarks that women should not use their recent successes to isolate themselves anew.

"I do not fully comprehend why women, who deplore men's old boy ways," she said, "nonetheless place extraordinarily high value on women's separation. My dream, which has been realized to a very great extent in my own life, is of men and women who, in combination, forge new patterns of career and parenthood."

Court Rejects an F.C.C. Curb on 'Indecency' in Broadcasts

BY STUART TAYLOR JR. | JULY 30, 1988

WASHINGTON, JULY 29 — A Federal appeals court ruled today that a Federal Communications Commission ban on the broadcasting of "indecent" language during evening hours violated the rights of free speech.

The three judges ruled that the commission had not shown that a ban in the evening hours was necessary to prevent substantial numbers of unsupervised children from seeing or hearing such material.

But the court upheld other aspects of the F.C.C.'s 1987 order restricting such broadcasts, including the ban on broadcasting "indecent" material between 6 A.M. and 10 A.M. The court also upheld the F.C.C. definition of such material as describing or depicting, "in terms patently offensive as measured by contemporary community standards for the broadcast medium, sexual or excretory activities and organs."

The case will now go back to the F.C.C., which must either return to 10 P.M. as the hour when broadcasters may begin to transmit indecent material, or produce stronger evidence for the contention that large numbers of unsupervised children would be exposed to such material between 10 P.M. and midnight.

POSSIBLE EFFECT ON SENATE ACTION

The decision casts doubt on the constitutionality of proposed legislation that the Senate adopted this week, which would require the commission to ban "indecent" programming 24 hours a day.

The F.C.C.'s 1987 order was intended to tighten its own previous restrictions, which had sought to shield children by banning the repetitious use of certain four-letter "dirty words" in broadcasts before 10 P.M. That order broadened the definition of indecent material and banned the broadcasting of such material before midnight.

The Supreme Court, in a 1978 decision, had ruled that the commission could ban as indecent the daytime broadcasting of a monologue by the comedian George Carlin, "Filthy Words," in order to shield children from such material.

Judge Ruth Bader Ginsburg's opinion today, in which Judges Spottswood W. Robinson 3d and David B. Sentelle joined, stressed that "broadcast material that is indecent but not obscene is protected by the First Amendment."

Judge Ginsburg said that the broadcast of such material to adults could not be restricted except insofar as necessary to shield unsupervised children, and that the commission's only basis for regulating such material "is not to establish itself as censor but to assist parents in controlling the material young children will hear."

BAN UNJUSTIFIED

Judge Ginsburg said the commission had not shown that enough unsupervised children would be exposed to such broadcasts during the evening hours before midnight to justify banning "indecent" broadcasts during those hours, or at least between 10 P.M. and midnight.

On the other hand, the court upheld the commission's ban on such programming between 6 A.M. and 10 A.M., including its warning to a New York City talk show, of which the host is Howard Stern, not to use indecent material during its 6 A.M. to 10 A.M. air time. The Stern show was one of several test cases in the issue of broadcasting indecent material in those morning hours.

The court overturned warnings given by the F.C.C. to the student-run radio station KCSB-FM in Santa Barbara, Calif., which broadcast the song "Makin' Bacon," and to a Pacifica Foundation Inc. radio station in Los Angeles, which broadcast a play entitled "Jerker," about the sexual fantasies of a homosexual man. Both broadcasts took place between 10 P.M. and midnight.

Judge Ginsburg did not specify the right time in the evening for the broadcast of "indecent" material, leaving that for the commission to determine in further proceedings, subject to further appeals.

VINDICATION IS SEEN

Timothy B. Dyk, a Washington lawyer representing a coalition of 17 plaintiffs in the case — including the three broadcasting networks and public interest groups including Action for Children's Television case — said today:

"It seems to me it's a substantial victory which vindicates the coalition's position that this is protected speech and that the adult audience should have access to it. The court held that the commission's sole interest here is to give parents the opportunity to supervise their children, and that rationale suggests possibly moving the hour even earlier than 10 P.M.

"This is not about sex talk on the telephone. We're talking about things that have very substantial literary and informational value, including some favorably reviewed plays that come potentially under this broad definition of indecency."

VICTORY IS CLAIMED

But Dennis R. Patrick, chairman of the commission, and Diane S. Killory, the general counsel, said their side had won.

"I do think that the commission got a substantial victory in this decision," Ms. Killory said. "The court affirmed our authority to regulate the broadcasting of indecent material so that parents can be sure that their children not be exposed to it."

Judge Ginsburg rejected arguments by various plaintiffs that the commission's definition of indecent material was unconstitutionally vague, holding that the 1978 Supreme Court decision foreclosed this argument.

She also rejected arguments that the definition was unconstitutionally broad because it restricted the times at which some material that has social value may be broadcast.

"The F.C.C. may regulate such material only with due respect for the high value our Constitution places on freedom of choice in what the people say and hear," the judge said, adding that it "must afford broadcasters clear notice of reasonably determined times at which indecent material safely may be aired."

CHAPTER 2

Life as a Justice

In 1993, Ginsburg was appointed as a Supreme Court justice for her impressive legal background and fair approach, striking a balance between the liberal left and conservative right. She became the second woman ever to serve in that position and the first Jewish justice since 1969. Her time in the Supreme Court, spanning over 25 years, has allowed her to oversee cases, participate in oral arguments and change the law to fit the circumstances and society we are currently living in, one case at a time.

Rejected as a Clerk, Chosen as a Justice: Ruth Joan Bader Ginsburg

BY NEIL A. LEWIS | JUNE 15, 1993

WASHINGTON, JUNE 14 — In 1960, a dean at the Harvard Law School, Albert Sachs, proposed one of his star students to Justice Felix Frankfurter of the Supreme Court as a law clerk. Justice Frankfurter told Professor Sachs that while the candidate was impressive, he just wasn't ready to hire a woman and so couldn't offer a job to Ruth Bader Ginsburg.

Judge Ginsburg, who now sits on the Federal appeals court and was chosen today by President Clinton for the Supreme Court, recently told that story to her own law clerks to explain how she became interested in the role of women in the eyes of the law.

FORCE BEFORE THE COURT

In the years between that rebuff by Justice Frankfurter and her appointment to the United States Court of Appeals for the District of Columbia Circuit in 1980, Ruth Ginsburg was a major force on the other side of the Supreme Court's high bench.

From 1973 to 1976 she argued six women's rights cases before the Court and won five of them, profoundly changing the law as it affects women.

"She is the Thurgood Marshall of gender equality law," said Janet Benshoof, the president of the Center for Reproductive Law and Policy, an abortion-rights advocacy group, repeating a common description of Judge Ginsburg. Like Justice Marshall, who shaped the legal strategy of the civil rights movement for the NAACP Legal and Educational Defense Fund before he joined the Court, Ruth Ginsburg organized the cases, found the plaintiffs and delivered the oral arguments.

As the director of the Women's Rights Project of the American Civil Liberties Union, Ms. Ginsburg adopted a strategy intended to convince the Justices that laws that discriminated between men and women — even those laws that were meant to help women — were based on unfair and harmful stereotypes and were in most cases unconstitutional. To do that, she often used men as plaintiffs, showing that both men and women suffered from such stereotypes.

"Her strategy was an especially ingenious one, relying on male, often married, plaintiffs," said David Cole, a professor at Georgetown University Law School who recently wrote a law review article discussing Ms. Ginsburg's approach to the Supreme Court.

He said many of the regulations or laws she opposed ostensibly helped women, giving them some extra benefit in recognition of the prevailing notion that women were generally dependent on men.

"But she set out to prove that those kinds of laws in fact harmed women by contributing to a stereotyped view of their role," he said.

The first case she argued and won before the Court, in 1973, involved a female Air Force lieutenant, Sharron Frontiero, and her husband, Joseph, who challenged a statute that treated male and female service members differently. Under the law, a serviceman could claim his wife as a dependent and qualify for increased housing even if she did not depend on his income, while a woman in uniform had to show that her husband received more than half his support from her to qualify for the extra housing allowance.

A NEW JURISPRUDENCE

In her brief and argument, Ms. Ginsburg presented the Court with an array of evidence that women were branded inferior through such treatment. The Justices voted 8 to 1 in her favor, embarking on the road to a new jurisprudence that made it harder for the law to treat women differently.

In 1976, in another case in which Ms. Ginsburg had filed a brief, the Justices set a standard that is still used today in sex discrimination cases. In that case, Craig v. Boren, the Court struck down an Oklahoma statute that said women as young as 18 could buy 3.2 percent beer while men had to be at least 21.

In its ruling, the Court declined to impose what is known as "strict scrutiny" of such discriminatory laws, which places a high burden on a state to justify making distinctions. But the Court did create a category known as "intermediate scrutiny," meaning that states could not enact laws that discriminated on the basis of sex without showing a substantial government interest.

Behind all the categorizing, the ruling's effect was to make it far harder to enact laws based on sexual stereotypes.

"Ruth Ginsburg was as responsible as any one person for legal advances that women made under the Equal Protection Clause of the Constitution," said Marcia Greenberger, the co-president of the National Women's Law Center. "As a result, doors of opportunity have been opened that have benefited not only the women themselves but their families."

REMEMBERING HER MOTHER

Ruth Joan Bader was born March, 15, 1933, in the Flatbush section of Brooklyn, and graduated from James Madison High School. Her father, Nathan Bader, owned small clothing stores. Her mother, Celia Bader, died of stomach cancer when Ruth was 17; at the White House today, Judge Ginsburg paid tribute to her mother.

At Cornell University, she met Martin D. Ginsburg, a fellow pre-law student, and they were married in June 1954, the same month she graduated from college. "They had a marvelous romance in her senior year," recalled a cousin, Jane Gevirtz of Manhattan.

Ms. Gevirtz said she recently came upon a letter that Ms. Ginsburg had written to her in 1953 in which she said she wanted to be a lawyer but had deep doubts on whether she had sufficient aptitude for the law. Ms. Gevirtz said her cousin nonetheless wrote that she was determined to see if she could get into law school, despite being told from all sides that it was more appropriate for a woman to be a teacher.

Her first child, Jane, was born the year after she married. Her aptitude for the law was sufficient for Harvard Law School, and she found herself caring for an infant and attending Harvard for the next two years.

When her husband found a job in New York, she transferred to Columbia Law School. Ms. Ginsburg was elected to the law reviews of both Harvard and Columbia.

Years later she became the first tenured female professor at Columbia University Law School, where her daughter, Jane, an authority on copyright law, is now on the faculty. She also has a son, James.

Mr. Ginsburg, an expert on tax law who has been Ross Perot's tax lawyer for years, was an economic adviser in Mr. Perot's Presidential campaign.

While Judge Ginsburg is modest in demeanor, even shy, her husband is an ebullient sort, friends said.

Despite her long record as a champion of women's rights, Judge Ginsburg has occasionally disappointed some of her former allies in the liberal advocacy groups. In her 13 years on the appeals court, she has often gone out of her way to mediate between the court's warring liberal and conservative factions.

But what has most dismayed some of her natural allies are her comments criticizing some aspects of Roe v. Wade, the 1973 Supreme Court ruling that declared there was a constitutional right to abortion.

In a speech in March at New York University, Judge Ginsburg outlined her objections to the 1973 ruling, which she said was too sweeping and thus contributed to the bitter debate over the last 20 years.

In essence, Judge Ginsburg argued that it was unwise of the Court majority to impose a detailed scheme prescribing how states may regulate abortion in each trimester of a pregnancy. Instead, she suggested, the Court should simply have overturned the law at issue, a Texas statute that outlawed nearly all abortions.

"Suppose the Court had stopped there, declaring unconstitutional the most extreme brand of law in the nation and had not gone on, as the Court did in Roe, to fashion a regime blanketing the subject," Ms. Ginsburg said, adding that a narrower ruling would have "served to reduce rather than to fuel controversy."

In that case, she went on, states would have more latitude to resolve the public dispute about abortion by creating their own abortion statutes, testing the Court's limits on how far they could go to restrict abortion.

Judge Ginsburg also said she believed the decision should have been grounded in a broad concept of equality for women. The Roe v. Wade decision was based instead on the idea that there is a constitutional right of privacy, which she did not discuss in the speech. Some abortion-rights advocates said today that the speech gave them concerns about her position in disputes over whether states can inhibit abortions with restrictions like waiting periods.

Kate Michelman, the president of the National Abortion Rights Action League, hinted at her group's displeasure with Judge Ginsburg's reservations about Roe. "Judge Ginsburg has been a strong advocate for women's equality," she said, "but her criticism of Roe v. Wade is cause for concern. We look forward to a thorough Senate Judiciary Committee hearing to determine whether Judge Ginsburg will protect a woman's fundamental right to privacy."

Supporters like Ms. Benshoof insist that Judge Ginsburg is a reliable supporter of abortion rights. In a 1989 opinion, in fact, Judge Ginsburg dissented from a ruling that allowed the Bush Administration to continue its policy of denying financing to international family planning groups that counsel abortion.

Transcript of President's Announcement and Judge Ginsburg's Remarks

SPECIAL TO THE NEW YORK TIMES | JUNE 15, 1993

WASHINGTON, JUNE 14 — Following is a transcript of remarks today by President Clinton and Judge Ruth Bader Ginsburg, as recorded by the Federal News Service, a transcription company:

BY PRESIDENT CLINTON

Please be seated. I wish you all a good afternoon, and I thank the members of the Congress and other interested Americans who are here. In just a few days when the Supreme Court concludes its term, Justice Byron White will begin a new chapter in his long and productive life. He has served the Court as he has lived, with distinction, intelligence, and honor. And he retires from public service with the deep gratitude of all the American people.

Article 2, Section 2 of the United States Constitution empowers the President to select a nominee to fill a vacancy on the Supreme Court of the United States. This responsibility is one of the most significant duties assigned to the President by the Constitution. A Supreme Court justice has life tenure, unlike the President, and along with his or her colleagues, decides the most significant questions of our time and shapes the continuing contours of our liberty.

I care a lot about this responsibility, not only because I am a lawyer, but because I used to teach constitutional law and I served my state as attorney general. I know well how the Supreme Court affects the lives of all Americans personally and deeply. I know clearly that a Supreme Court justice should have the heart and spirit, the talent and discipline, the knowledge, common sense, and wisdom to translate the hopes of the American people as presented in the cases before it into an enduring body of constitutional law, constitutional law that will preserve our most cherished values that are enshrined in that Constitution and at the same time enable the American people to move forward.

That is what I promised the American people in a justice when I ran for President, and I believe it is a promise that I am delivering on today. After careful reflection, I am proud to nominate for associate justice of the Supreme Court Judge Ruth Bader Ginsburg of the United States Court of Appeals to the District of Columbia. I will send her name to the Senate to fill the vacancy created by Justice White's retirement. As I told Judge Ginsburg last night when I called to ask her to accept the nomination, I decided on her for three reasons.

First, in her years on the bench, she has genuinely distinguished herself as one of our nation's best judges, progressive in outlook, wise in judgment, balanced and fair in her opinions.

Second, over the course of a lifetime in her pioneering work in behalf of the women of this country, she has compiled a truly historic record of achievement in the finest traditions of American law and citizenship.

And, finally, I believe that in the years ahead, she will be able to be a force for consensus-building on the Supreme Court, just as she has been on the Court of Appeals, so that our judges can become an instrument of our common unity in the expression of their fidelity to the Constitution.

Nominee's Background

Judge Ginsburg received her undergraduate degree from Cornell. She attended both Harvard and Columbia law schools and served on the law reviews of both institutions, the first woman to have earned this distinction. She was a law clerk to a Federal judge, a law professor at Rutgers and Columbia law schools. She argued six landmark cases in behalf of women before the United States Supreme Court and, happily, won five out of six.

For the past 13 years, she has served on the United States Court of Appeals for the District of Columbia, the second-highest court in our country, where her work has brought her national acclaim, and on which she was able to amass a record that caused a national legal journal in 1991 to name her as one the nation's leading centrist judges.

In the months and years ahead, the country will have the opportunity to get to know much more about Ruth Ginsburg's achievements, decency, humanity and fairness. People will find, as I have, that this nominee is a person of immense character. Quite simply, what's in her record speaks volumes about what is in her heart. Throughout her life, she has repeatedly stood for the individual, the person less well off, the outsider in society, and has given those people greater hope by telling them that they have a place in our legal system, by giving them a sense that the Constitution and the laws protect all the American people, not simply the powerful.

Judge Ginsburg has also proven herself to be a healer, what attorneys call a moderate. Time and again, her moral imagination has cooled the fires of her colleagues' discord, ensuring that the right of jurists to dissent ennobles the law without entangling the court.

The announcement of this vacancy brought forth a unique outpouring for support from distinguished Americans on Judge Ginsburg's behalf. What caused that outpouring is the essential quality of the Judge herself, her deep respect for others and her willingness to subvert self interest to the interests of our people and their institutions.

In one of her own writings about what it is like to be a justice, Judge Ginsburg quotes Justice Louis Brandeis who once said, "The Supreme Court is not a place for solo performers." If this is a time for consensus-building on the Court, and I believe it is, Judge Ginsburg will be an able and effective architect of that effort.

Advocacy for Women

It is important to me that Judge Ginsburg came to her views and attitudes by doing, not merely by reading and studying. Despite her enormous ability and academic achievements, she could not get a job with a law firm in the early 1960's because she was a woman and the mother of a small child. Having experienced discrimination, she devoted the next 20 years of her career to fighting it and making this country a better place for our wives, our mothers, our sisters and our daughters.

She herself argued and won many of the women's-rights cases before the Supreme Court in the 1970's. Many admirers of her work say that she is to the women's movement what former Supreme Court Justice Thurgood Marshall was to the movement for the rights of African-Americans. I can think of no greater compliment to bestow on an American lawyer. And she has done all of this, and a lot of other things as well, while raising a family with her husband, Marty, who she married 39 years ago as a very young woman. Together they had two children, Jane and James, and they now have two grandchildren. Hers is a remarkable record of distinction and achievement both professional and personal.

During the selection process, we reviewed the qualifications of more than 40 potential nominees. It was a long, exhaustive search, and during that time we identified several wonderful Americans whom I think could be outstanding nominees to the Supreme Court in the future.

Among the best were the Secretary of the Interior, Bruce Babbitt, whose strong legal background as Arizona's Attorney General and recent work balancing the competing interests of environmentalists and others in the very difficult issues affecting the American West made him a highly qualified candidate for the Court. And I had the unusual experience — something unique to me — of being flooded with calls across America from Babbitt admirers who pleaded with me not to put him on the Court and take him away from the Interior Department.

I also carefully considered the chief judge of the First Circuit, Judge Stephen Breyer of Boston, a man whose character, competence and legal scholarship impressed me very greatly. I believe he has a very major role to play in public life, I believe he is superbly qualified to be on the Court, and I think either one of these candidates, as well as the handful of others whom I closely considered, may well find themselves in that position some day in the future.

Let me say in closing that Ruth Bader Ginsburg cannot be called a liberal or a conservative. She has proved herself too thoughtful for such labels. As she herself put it in one of her articles, and I quote: "The greatest figures of the American judiciary have been independent thinking individuals with open but not empty minds — individuals willing to listen and to learn. They have exhibited a readiness to re-examine their own premises — liberal or conservative — as thoroughly as those of others."

That, I believe, describes Judge Ginsburg, and those I, too, believe are the qualities of a great justice. If, as I believe, the measure of a person's values can best be measured by examining the life the person lives, then Judge Ginsburg's values are the very ones that represent the best in America.

I am proud to nominate this path-breaking attorney, advocate and judge, to be the 107th justice to the United States Supreme Court.

BY JUDGE GINSBURG

Mr. President, I am grateful beyond measure for the confidence you have placed in me, and I will strive with all that I have to live up to your expectations in making this appointment.

I appreciate, too, the special caring of Senator Daniel Patrick Moynihan, the more so because I do not actually know the Senator. I was born and brought up in New York, the state Senator Moynihan represents, and he was the very first person to call with good wishes when President Carter nominated me in 1980 to serve on the U.S. Court of Appeals for the District of Columbia Circuit. Senator Moynihan has offered the same encouragement on this occasion.

May I introduce at this happy moment three people very special to me: my husband, Martin B. Ginsburg, my son-in-law, George T. Spera Jr., and my son, James Steven Ginsburg.

The announcement the President just made is significant, I believe, because it contributes to the end of the days when women, at least half the talent pool in our society, appear in high places only as one-at-a-time performers. Recall that when President Carter took office in 1976, no woman ever served on the Supreme Court, and only one woman, Shirley Hufstedler of California, then served at the next Federal court level, the United States Court of Appeals.

Today Justice Sandra Day O'Connor graces the Supreme Court bench, and close to 25 women serve at the Federal Court of Appeals level, two as chief judges. I am confident that more will soon join them. That seems to me inevitable, given the change in law school enrollment.

Views on the Judiciary

My law school class in the late 1950's numbered over 500. That class included less than 10 women. As the President said, not a law firm in the entire city of New York bid for my employment as a lawyer when I earned my degree. Today few law schools have female enrollment under 40 percent, and several have reached or passed the 50 percent mark. And thanks to Title VII, no entry doors are barred.

My daughter, Jane, reminded me a few hours ago in a good-luck call from Australia of a sign of the change we have had the good fortune to experience. In her high school yearbook on her graduation in 1973, the listing for Jane Ginsburg under "ambition" was "to see her mother appointed to the Supreme Court." The next line read, "If necessary, Jane will appoint her." Jane is so pleased, Mr. President, that you did it instead, and her brother, James, is, too.

I expect to be asked in some detail about my views of the work of a good judge on a High Court bench. This afternoon is not the moment for extended remarks on that subject, but I might state a few prime guides.

Chief Justice Rehnquist offered one I keep in the front of my mind: a judge is bound to decide each case fairly in a court with the relevant facts and the applicable law even when the decision is not, as he put it, what the home crowd wants.

Next, I know no better summary than the one Justice O'Connor recently provided drawn from a paper by New York University Law School Prof. Bert Neuborne. The remarks concern the enduring influence of Justice Oliver Wendell Holmes. They read: "When a modern constitutional judge is confronted with a hard case, Holmes is at her side with three gentle reminders: first, intellectual honesty about the available policy choices; second, disciplined self-restraint in respecting the majority's policy choice; and third, principled commitment to defense of individual autonomy even in the face of majority action." To that I can only say, "Amen."

I am indebted to so many for this extraordinary chance and challenge: to a revived women's movement in the 1970's that opened doors for people like me, to the civil rights movement of the 1960's from which the women's movement drew inspiration, to my teaching colleagues at Rutgers and Columbia and for 13 years my D.C. Circuit colleagues who shaped and heightened my appreciation of the value of collegiality.

Gratitude to Family

Most closely, I have been aided by my life partner, Martin D. Ginsburg, who has been, since our teen-age years, my best friend and biggest booster, by my mother-in-law, Evelyn Ginsburg, the most supportive parent a person could have, and by a daughter and son with the tastes to appreciate that Daddy cooks ever so much better than Mommy and so phased me out of the kitchen at a relatively early age.

Finally, I know Hillary Rodham Clinton has encouraged and supported the President's decision to utilize the skills and talents of all the people of the United States. I did not, until today, know Mrs. Clinton, but I hasten to add that I am not the first member of my family to stand close to her. There is another I love dearly to whom the First Lady is already an old friend. My wonderful granddaughter, Clara witnessed this super, unposed photograph taken last October when Mrs. Clinton visited the nursery school in New York and led the little ones in "The Toothbrush Song." The small person right in front is Clara.

I have a last thank-you. It is to my mother, Celia Amster Bader, the bravest and strongest person I have known, who was taken from me much too soon. I pray that I may be all that she would have been had she lived in an age when women could aspire and achieve and daughters are cherished as much as sons. I look forward to stimulating weeks this summer and, if I am confirmed, to working at a neighboring court to the best of my ability for the advancement of the law in the service of society. Thank you.

QUESTION AND ANSWER

Q: *The withdrawal of the Guinier nomination, sir, and your apparent focus on Judge Breyer, and your turn, late it seems, to Judge Ginsburg, may have created an impression, perhaps unfair, of a certain zigzag quality in the decision-making process here. I wonder, sir, if you could kind of walk us through it, perhaps disabuse us of any notion we might have along those lines. Thank you.*

PRESIDENT CLINTON I have long since given up the thought that I could disabuse some of you turning any substantive decision into anything but political process. How you could ask a question like that after the statement she just made is beyond me.

The Man Behind the High Court Nominee

BY STEPHEN LABATON | JUNE 17, 1993

WASHINGTON, JUNE 16 — In 1980, a handful of Republican senators appeared to be reluctant to confirm another Carter appointment to a Federal Court in an election year, so the prospective judge's husband mentioned the problem to a client.

The husband, Martin D. Ginsburg, told the client, Ross Perot, along with other influential friends in academic and political and corporate circles.

The senators were called.

And in the end, only one Republican on the Judiciary Committee, Senator Strom Thurmond of South Carolina, voted against Ruth Bader Ginsburg's nomination to join the Federal Court of Appeals in Washington.

EXTRAORDINARY RECORD

Even though she had established an extraordinary record as a lawyer and teacher, Ms. Ginsburg has acknowledged that without the strong personal and political support of her husband, she may never have become President Clinton's choice for the Supreme Court.

For his part, Mr. Ginsburg said in an interview today: "I have been supportive of my wife since the beginning of time, and she has been supportive of me. It's not sacrifice; it's family."

It was also a sign of the changing times that Mr. Ginsburg would have to leave behind a successful career as a lawyer and tenured tax professor at Columbia Law School in New York and move to Washington so that his wife could become a Federal judge here 13 years ago. When Mr. Ginsburg graduated from law school 35 years ago, his new bride transferred from Harvard to Columbia Law School so he could take a job as an associate at a Manhattan law firm.

As women have begun to reach the highest ranks of political and judicial power, Mr. Ginsburg has come to represent a new kind of spouse: the husband as alter ego, adviser and political booster. It is a kind of role reversal that has been performed in recent months by Michael Kramer, the journalist who promoted the candidacy of his wife, Judge Kimba M. Wood, for Attorney General. Judge Wood was dropped by the White House after it was learned that the couple had employed an illegal immigrant to care for their son (although doing so was legal at the time).

Friends say Mr. Ginsburg worked behind the scenes to help persuade Mr. Clinton to nominate Judge Ginsburg for the Supreme Court, calling on leading scholars to write to Mr. Clinton and his counsel, Bernard W. Nussbaum.

When rumors began circulating last month that Judge Ginsburg had opposed the right to abortion, Mr. Ginsburg enlisted academics to tell the White House and others that his wife had criticized the reasoning, but not the result, of the 1973 case establishing the constitutional right.

And in a capital that has grown hypersensitive to the tax histories of nominees for high office, it was Mr. Ginsburg, one of the nation's leading tax experts, who averted any controversy about the couple's finances. On a few hours' notice, Mr. Ginsburg compiled years of financial records over the weekend. He walked Government accountants through years of filings on Sunday, as Mr. Nussbaum was interviewing Judge Ginsburg in another room of the couple's Watergate apartment on a variety of legal and personal issues.

DEDUCTION DEFENDED

When the Government accountants on Sunday challenged a $100 deduction, the tax professor who had structured some of the most complex corporate transactions was able to defend the accounting easily.

The financial records of the couple were significantly simplified by Mr. Ginsburg's decision in 1980 to sell all of his stock so that his wife would not have to remove herself from cases involving companies or industries in which the family had interests.

Mr. Ginsburg played down his role in the nomination, saying he spoke to only a few legal scholars he knew and only after a friend at the White House asked him, "What have you done about generating support from the academics?"

He said he was told: "Given that her background was as a scholar, if the world doesn't generate at least seven letters from academics then the White House will get very nervous."

The letters poured in — from politicians like Gov. Ann W. Richards of Texas and legal scholars like the presidents of Stanford and Columbia (both former law school deans). A number were not directly solicited by Mr. Ginsburg, who said what he did was merely repeat what he was told by the White House friend whom he declined to identify.

President Clinton said today that he was not influenced by the letters and that they showed "only that a lot of people felt a lot for her."

Mr. Ginsburg, 61 years old, was born in Brooklyn and raised in Rockville Centre, L.I. Through mutual friends, he met Ruth Bader at Cornell, and after his two-year service in the Army and the birth of their daughter, they enrolled a year apart at Harvard Law School. While she was developing a whole new area of law involving equal rights for women, he practiced tax law.

He decided to teach full time in 1977, when he did a stint at Stanford Law School. He sought that job to be with his wife, who had been invited to be a resident fellow for a term at Stanford's Center for Advanced Study in Behavioral Sciences.

In 1971, Mr. Ginsburg met Ross Perot when his law firm represented Mr. Perot in a deal, and the friendship blossomed. He did not work on Mr. Perot's Presidential campaign, although he spoke with his economic adviser, John White, on some issues. Mr. Ginsburg said he had supported Mr. Clinton.

By all accounts, Mr. Perot grew particularly close to Mr. Ginsburg after the lawyer resolved a thicket of thorny tax problems that had threatened the acquisition of Mr. Perot's Electronic Data Systems Inc. by the General Motors Corporation in 1984.

Mr. Ginsburg hesitated before taking the assignment because his law firm represented several of Mr. Perot's competitors. While technically it was not a conflict of interest, Mr. Ginsburg said, "It looked unseemly."

But his long friendship with Mr. Perot, combined with his intellectual interest in completing one of the most challenging mergers, prompted him to do the job. To ease tensions with his law firm, he told Mr. Perot that he would work without pay.

Ultimately, he said, Mr. Perot said he wanted to repay Mr. Ginsburg some way, and after the deal was completed his client said he would endow a chair at any university Mr. Ginsburg liked.

UNWANTED MONUMENT

"I said, 'It's a bad idea,' " Mr. Ginsburg recalled. "Endowed chairs are only for dead people."

But Mr. Perot said if Mr. Ginsburg did not pick a school, then the money would go to Oral Roberts University.

"Ross said when the founder of Oral Roberts heard it was to be the Martin D. Ginsburg chair, he took a deep breath and then said, 'Well, Ross, we're all God's children.' "

In the end, the money went to Georgetown University Law Center, where Mr. Ginsburg had been teaching since 1980. But Mr. Ginsburg has not filled the chair, because, he said, he is superstitious, and the interest on the endowment has been used to pay for books at the law school library.

On a shelf in the family's Watergate apartment sits a gift from some of Judge Ginsburg's clerks: a six-inch piece of furniture with a small plaque that identifies it as the Martin D. Ginsburg chair.

Ginsburg Promises Judicial Restraint if She Joins Court

BY NEIL A. LEWIS | JULY 21, 1993

WASHINGTON, JULY 20 — Judge Ruth Bader Ginsburg, President Clinton's nominee to the Supreme Court, told the Senate Judiciary Committee today that she would be neither a conservative nor a liberal on the Court, but someone who ruled cautiously, without reaching out to write broad principles into the law.

In her opening statement to the committee, which began its hearings today on the nomination, Judge Ginsburg also sought to set a clear boundary on what kind of questions she was willing to answer. She said she would not discuss specific cases or issues that might come before her.

"It would be wrong for me to say or preview in this legislative chamber how I would cast my vote on questions the Supreme Court may be called upon to decide," she said. "A judge sworn to decide impartially can offer no forecasts, no hints, for that would show not only disregard for the specifics of the particular case, it would display disdain for the entire judicial process."

CONFIRMATION APPEARS SURE

Although such unwillingness to engage in specifics has frustrated and annoyed some senators in the past, it was clear today that it will make no difference for Judge Ginsburg, who seems bound to win Senate approval easily.

If confirmed as the nation's 107th Justice, Judge Ginsburg, the 60-year-old member of the United States Court of Appeals for the District of Columbia Circuit, would become the second woman on the Court, joining Justice Sandra Day O'Connor, who was sworn in in 1981. She would also be the first justice placed on the court by a Democrat in 26 years.

In a colloquy with Senator Howard M. Metzenbaum, Democrat of Ohio, Judge Ginsburg noted with approval that in a case last year from Pennsylvania, the Supreme Court reaffirmed the constitutional right to abortion. But she pointedly declined to say whether she believed it was a fundamental right, a category that would mean it would be difficult for states to enact restrictions on abortion.

"Now what regulations are going to be permitted is certainly a question that is going to be before this court," she said. "And that depends in part, Senator, on the kind of record that's presented to the court, and I don't feel it would be appropriate for me to go beyond the point of repeating what the majority of the court has said, that this is a right of women guaranteed by the 14th Amendment."

VIEW ON ROE DEFENDED

Judge Ginsburg also defended her view, as expressed in law reviews and speeches, that Roe v. Wade, the 1973 ruling that first found a constitutional right to abortion went too far, too fast.

She said that in her writings she had engaged in a "what if?" kind of speculation. Had the Court not set down so detailed a scheme prescribing the way states may regulate abortion in each of the three trimesters of pregnancy, there would have not been so much controversy.

After Roe, she said, the abortion-rights movement became complacent "because the court seemed to have taken care of the problem and the other side had a target around which to rally."

She said, "I could be wrong," but that she believed that had Roe not been so specific, state legislatures would have gradually enacted laws that would have been more enduring than Roe.

Several committee members addressed Judge Ginsburg as if her confirmation were a foregone conclusion.

Senator Carol Moseley Braun, Democrat of Illinois, called her a "brilliant jurist and legal scholar" and said she hoped that Justice Ginsburg would assume the mantle of retired justices William B.

Brennan Jr. and Thurgood Marshall. "I say that without prejudging this nomination, kind of," she said to laughter.

CAUTION FROM SPECTER

Senator Paul Simon, also an Illinois Democrat, said he believed Judge Ginsburg would be confirmed unanimously.

Senator Arlen Specter, a Pennsylvania Republican who returned to work Monday after surgery to remove a benign brain tumor, sounded the only cautionary note. Wearing a baseball cap to conceal his bandaged head, he complained that the committee was not taking its role seriously enough because everyone presumed that Judge Ginsburg would be confirmed no matter what.

In her remarks to the 18-member committee, Judge Ginsburg sought to emphasize her commitment to judicial restraint.

"Let me try to state in a nutshell how I view the work of judging," she said. "My approach, I believe, is neither liberal nor conservative."

She quoted Alexander Hamilton as saying a judge should administer the law impartially. "I would add that the judge should carry out that function without fanfare, but with due care" she said. "She should decide the case before her without reaching out to cover cases not yet seen.

"She should be ever mindful, as Judge and then Justice Benjamin Nathan Cardozo said: 'Justice is not to be taken by storm. She is to be wooed by slow advance.' "

BROOKLYN PAST EVOKED

Judge Ginsburg's opening statement was also a testament to the evolution of modern confirmation hearings, as some of her remarks showed how the White House has absorbed lessons from recent past appearances before the committee.

In 1991, Judge Clarence Thomas impressed the committee and the nation with his opening statement, describing how he overcame a childhood of crushing poverty in the town of Pinpoint, Ga., to go on to college and Yale Law School and eventually a seat on a Federal appeals court. The approach became known as Judge Thomas's "Pin-point Strategy."

Judge Ginsburg included in her statement what might be called her "Flatbush Strategy," briefly discussing her upbringing in the Brooklyn neighborhood. Her grandparents, she said, left Europe, where their Judaism subjected them to, "pogroms and denigration of one's human worth." Her parents instilled in her a love of learning, she said.

In 1987, Judge Robert H. Bork was strongly criticized for his answer to a question on the reason he wanted to be on the Supreme Court. His response that he regarded the position as "an intellectual feast" seemed to bolster the notion pressed by his opponents that he was an unfeeling and thus unsuitable candidate for the Supreme Court.

Judge Ginsburg sought to pre-empt that question today, saying she wanted to be on the Court to help people.

"It is an opportunity beyond any other for one of my training to serve society," she said. "The controversies that come before the Supreme Court as the last judicial resort touch and concern the health and well-being of our nation and its people."

Before being named to the appeals court 13 years ago by President Jimmy Carter, Ruth Bader Ginsburg was a leading litigator of women's rights cases, arguing six cases before the Supreme Court and winning all but one.

In discussing her strategy of persuading the all-male Court of the early 1970's to accept her arguments, Judge Ginsburg said she saw herself as much as a teacher as an advocate.

"I was trying to educate them that there was something wrong," she said. "One of the differences about gender discrimination and race discrimination was that race discrimination was immediately perceived as evil, odious and intolerable. But the response that I got from the judges before whom I argued when I talked about sex discrimination was: 'What are you talking about? Women are treated ever so much better than men.' "

Senate, 96-3, Easily Affirms Judge Ginsburg as a Justice

BY LINDA GREENHOUSE | AUG. 4, 1993

WASHINGTON, AUG. 3 — Ruth Bader Ginsburg easily won confirmation to the Supreme Court today, and within hours of the Senate vote Judge Ginsburg, who argued six cases before the Justices as an advocate for women's rights, returned to the Court to inspect her new office.

Judge Ginsburg, who was on the United States Court of Appeals for the District of Columbia Circuit, will officially become Justice Ginsburg when she takes the oath of office next Tuesday. She arrived at the Court in midafternoon in a silver Nissan Maxima driven by her husband, Martin. "It feels wonderful," she said of her confirmation as the car paused briefly before disappearing into the Court's underground garage.

The purpose of the visit was to discuss the logistics of her impending move into chambers being vacated by Justice Clarence Thomas. Justice Thomas in turn will move into the chambers long occupied by Justice Byron R. White, who retired in June and whom Judge Ginsburg is succeeding.

Aside from a slight bustle caused by her visit, the building was quiet today: the Court is in recess and several of the Justices are out of town.

FLOOD OF NEW PAPERWORK

Work is piling up for Judge Ginsburg. She must familiarize herself with the 46 cases the Court has scheduled for argument in the term that begins on Oct. 4, as well as with the more than 1,000 new appeals the Court will dispose of on that date. Judge Ginsburg met with Francis J. Lorson, the chief deputy clerk, to discuss how to handle the flood of new paperwork.

She was confirmed this morning by a vote of 96 to 3. The only votes against her came from three conservative Republicans: Jesse Helms of North Carolina, Don Nickles of Oklahoma and Robert C. Smith of

Judge Ruth Bader Ginsburg visiting with Senator Joe Biden, chairman of the Judiciary committee, this past June.

New Hampshire. Senator Donald W. Riegle Jr., a Michigan Democrat, did not appear for the vote.

There was no debate on the Senate floor today. During a brief debate on Monday, Senator Helms said he had tentatively decided to vote in favor of Judge Ginsburg until he reviewed her record over the weekend. He contended that she supports the right to abortion unreservedly, and "is likely to uphold the homosexual agenda."

'WISE AND INSIGHTFUL' CHOICE

Senator Joseph R. Biden Jr., Democrat of Delaware, said Judge Ginsburg's nomination had been "one of the real joys" of his tenure as chairman of the Senate Judiciary Committee, which unanimously endorsed the nomination last week. He also said he hoped President Clinton would be "as wise and insightful" in choosing any future Supreme Court nominees.

Judge Ginsburg will be the second woman to sit on the Supreme Court, after Justice Sandra Day O'Connor, who was named to the Court by President Ronald Reagan in 1981, and is the first successful nominee by a Democratic President since Lyndon B. Johnson chose Thurgood Marshall in 1967.

She also will be the first Jewish Justice since Abe Fortas resigned in 1969, and the first native New Yorker to serve on the Court since Benjamin N. Cardozo, who died in office in 1938.

Federal judges take two oaths of office: the constitutional oath administered to all Federal employees, and a special judicial oath. The tentative schedule for Judge Ginsburg's swearing-in next week calls for her to take the first oath at the White House and the second in a private ceremony at the Court, with a public celebration to be held in October after the Court begins its new term.

After her Court visit, Judge Ginsburg went to the White House for a Rose Garden appearance with Mr. Clinton. Standing by her side in the 89-degree heat, the President predicted that she would be "a great Justice" who would "move the Court not left or right, but forward."

Inviting questions, Judge Ginsburg got this one: "You've been called a liberal, you've been called a conservative, you've been called a moderate. What are you?"

Borrowing pointedly from the Gilbert and Sullivan operetta "Iolanthe," she replied, to the apparent confusion of the White House press corps, "I don't believe that every child that's born alive is either a little liberal or else a little conservative, except in Gilbert and Sullivan."

Ginsburg at Fore in Court's Give-and-Take

BY LINDA GREENHOUSE | OCT. 14, 1993

WASHINGTON, OCT. 13 — The Supreme Court wrestled with two of the term's most important discrimination cases today, and for many minutes during the two intense hours of argument it was Justice Ruth Bader Ginsburg's courtroom.

The newest Justice, who spent the first part of her legal career fighting and helping to define sex discrimination, brought some of an advocate's passion to the day's arguments.

IN PLAIN ENGLISH

One case asks the Court to decide what constitutes sexual harassment on the job. The question in the other case is whether the Civil Rights Act of 1991, which strengthened the basic Federal law against employment discrimination, should be applied retroactively to lawsuits that were pending when it took effect.

Justice Ginsburg prodded and challenged the lawyers on both sides of the cases, managing to make her own point of view quite clear in plain-spoken alternatives to their sometimes convoluted legal formulations.

In the sexual harassment case, for example, she broke in as the argument stalled over such questions as whether to define sexual harassment from the point of view of a "reasonable woman" or "reasonable person," or whether the employer's conduct should be measured by some objective standard or on the basis of its impact on the woman bringing the suit.

Justice Ginsburg asked why sexual harassment should not be defined simply as conduct that on the basis of an employee's sex makes it more difficult for one person than another to perform the job. "How about just saying that?" she said. "Is it really more complex?

The terms and conditions of employment are not equal if one person is being called names and the other isn't."

Sexual harassment could be found if "one sex has to put up with something that the other sex doesn't have to put up with," she said at another point.

To one lawyer who was arguing that the Civil Rights Act of 1991 should not be given retroactive effect because it would be unfair to subject employers to the higher damage limits of the new law, she said there had been no change in the law's underlying principle. "Thou shalt not discriminate," she said. "That rule has been there all along. All that has been done is to make the price tag higher."

"You're not really suggesting, are you," she said to the lawyer, Glen D. Nager, that because the old law provided only limited remedies for discrimination, employers had felt free to disregard it.

'INFORMED JUDGMENTS'

Mr. Nager, representing two employers in the retroactivity case, said he was not relying on that argument to win his case. But he said employers did make "informed judgments," depending on the possible penalties for losing lawsuits, about how much money to spend to train their work force to avoid discrimination.

Since the 1991 law made new remedies available for successful civil rights plaintiffs, including compensatory and punitive damages, Mr. Nager said clients of his law firm had been calling for advice on holding seminars for their employees. The old Federal law against employment discrimination limited the remedies to injunctions against continued discrimination and back pay for lost wages.

Justice Ginsburg was scarcely the only member of the Court to take an active role in today's arguments. Every Justice asked questions with the exception of Justices Harry A. Blackmun and Clarence Thomas. Justice Antonin Scalia made his own view on the retroactivity issue abundantly clear.

"I had thought we had a rule, a long tradition from the common law, that retroactivity is disfavored," Justice Scalia said to Eric Schnapper, a lawyer with the NAACP Legal Defense and Educational Fund Inc. Mr. Schnapper was arguing that the 1991 law should apply to cases that were already in the legal pipeline when it took effect. There are thousands of discrimination cases in that category.

The text of the 1991 law says nothing about its effect on pending cases, the silence resulting from an impasse between the Democratic leadership in Congress, which favored retroactivity, and the Bush Administration, which adamantly opposed it.

SWIPES AT CONGRESS

Everyone in the courtroom knew the tortured history of the law, which Congress passed in part to counter the effect of a series of Supreme Court decisions in 1989 that narrowed the scope of existing civil rights laws. So there were audible chuckles after Mr. Nager opened his argument against retroactivity by saying that "this case would no doubt be easier" if Congress had dealt explicitly with the question and Justice Scalia commented with a straight face, "Maybe it slipped their mind."

Mr. Nager asked the Court to rule that unless Congress explicitly provided for retroactive application of a new law, the law could be applied only prospectively. "What Congress needs from this Court is clear direction, a rule it can understand," Mr. Nager said.

RARE HARASSMENT HEARING

Justice John Paul Stevens said, "There is a clear rule already," adding that whatever instructions Congress had given on the subject would have been enforced by the courts.

"It's clear that if they make it clear, we'll follow it," Justice Stevens said. "But it's not clear that if they don't make it clear, we won't follow it. That's what the one-upsmanship is all about."

Solicitor General Drew S. Days 3d, making his first Supreme Court argument on behalf of the Clinton Administration, asked the Court to find the 1991 law retroactive on the ground that it provided only new remedies without changing the underlying legal obligation not to discriminate. "The distinction is between imposing new obligations and providing new remedies for old wrongs," he said.

The sexual harassment case is only the Court's second case to deal with the subject. In the first case, seven years ago, the Court ruled unanimously that sexual harassment on the job is an aspect of employment discrimination that is prohibited by the Civil Rights Act of 1964.

In that case, Meritor Savings Bank v. Vinson, the Court defined sexual harassment as an "abusive working environment" that is so "severe or pervasive" as to "alter the conditions" of the victim's employment. That definition's imprecision has created confusion in the lower Federal courts over how to apply it.

In the case before the Court today, Harris v. Forklift Systems, the United States Court of Appeals for the Sixth Circuit, in Cincinnati, ruled that a plaintiff in a sexual harassment case had to prove that she suffered "severe psychological injury."

Applying that standard, the appeals court dismissed a case brought by a Nashville woman, Teresa Harris, against the owner of the truck leasing company where she worked as a manager. The owner had subjected her to derogatory comments such as, "You're a woman, what do you know?" He told her: "Let's go to the Holiday Inn to negotiate your raise." The court found that the employer, Charles Hardy, had been "vulgar" and crude but that Ms. Harris had not suffered enough to be able to bring a lawsuit.

Addressing Irwin Venick, Ms. Harris's lawyer, Chief Justice William H. Rehnquist asked whether the case would be any different if the employer had directed similar derogatory comments to men.

After Mr. Venick replied that there would not be a sexual harassment case if men and women were treated equally, Justice Ginsburg said that was not necessarily so. It is "hard to transpose" the two situations, she said, adding that " 'you're a woman and what do you know?' means something different than 'you're a man, what do you know?' "

Justice Scalia said to Mr. Venick: "You've never had anyone tell you that you're a man, so what do you know? You must live in a different family environment than I do."

Mr. Venick replied that he had heard such comments "not only in my family, but in the courtroom too."

DEFENDANT DROPS AN ARGUMENT

The employer in this case is no longer defending the Sixth Circuit's standard of severe psychological injury, so the Court spent no time discussing it. The company's lawyer, Stanley M. Chernau, said he agreed with Ms. Harris's lawyer that the requirement of showing psychological injury was too stringent a standard.

It appeared highly likely that the Court would overturn the appeals court's ruling and give Ms. Harris a new chance to prove her case. But it was much less clear what standard the Justices would settle on.

Court Is 'One of Most Activist,' Ginsburg Says, Vowing to Stay

BY ADAM LIPTAK | AUG. 24, 2013

WASHINGTON — Justice Ruth Bader Ginsburg, 80, vowed in an interview to stay on the Supreme Court as long as her health and intellect remained strong, saying she was fully engaged in her work as the leader of the liberal opposition on what she called "one of the most activist courts in history."

In wide-ranging remarks in her chambers on Friday that touched on affirmative action, abortion and same-sex marriage, Justice Ginsburg said she had made a mistake in joining a 2009 opinion that laid the groundwork for the court's decision in June effectively striking down the heart of the Voting Rights Act of 1965. The recent decision, she said, was "stunning in terms of activism."

Unless they have a book to sell, Supreme Court justices rarely give interviews. Justice Ginsburg has given several this summer, perhaps in reaction to calls from some liberals that she step down in time for President Obama to name her successor.

On Friday, she said repeatedly that the identity of the president who would appoint her replacement did not figure in her retirement planning.

"There will be a president after this one, and I'm hopeful that that president will be a fine president," she said.

Were Mr. Obama to name Justice Ginsburg's successor, it would presumably be a one-for-one liberal swap that would not alter the court's ideological balance. But if a Republican president is elected in 2016 and gets to name her successor, the court would be fundamentally reshaped.

Justice Ginsburg has survived two bouts with cancer, but her health is now good, she said, and her work ethic exceptional. There is no question, on the bench or in chambers, that she has full command of the complex legal issues that reach the court.

Her age has required only minor adjustments.

Justice Ruth Bader Ginsburg, in her chambers on Friday, said she hoped that some of her sharp dissents "will one day be the law."

"I don't water-ski anymore," Justice Ginsburg said. "I haven't gone horseback riding in four years. I haven't ruled that out entirely. But water-skiing, those days are over."

Justice Ginsburg, who was appointed by President Bill Clinton in 1993, said she intended to stay on the court "as long as I can do the job full steam, and that, at my age, is not predictable."

"I love my job," she added. "I thought last year I did as well as in past terms."

With the departure of Justice John Paul Stevens in 2010, Justice Ginsburg became the leader of the court's four-member liberal wing, a role she seems to enjoy. "I am now the most senior justice when we divide 5-4 with the usual suspects," she said.

The last two terms, which brought major decisions on Mr. Obama's health care law, race and same-sex marriage, were, she said, "heady, exhausting, challenging."

She was especially critical of the voting rights decision, as well as the part of the ruling upholding the health care law that nonetheless said it could not be justified under Congress's power to regulate interstate commerce.

In general, Justice Ginsburg said, "if it's measured in terms of readiness to overturn legislation, this is one of the most activist courts in history."

The next term, which begins on Oct. 7, is also likely to produce major decisions, she said, pointing at piles of briefs in cases concerning campaign contribution limits and affirmative action.

There is a framed copy of the Lilly Ledbetter Fair Pay Act of 2009 on a wall in her chambers. It is not a judicial decision, of course, but Justice Ginsburg counts it as one of her proudest achievements.

The law was a reaction to her dissent in Ledbetter v. Goodyear Tire and Rubber Company, the 2007 ruling that said Title VII of the Civil Rights Act of 1964 imposed strict time limits for bringing workplace discrimination suits. She called on Congress to overturn the decision, and it did.

"I'd like to think that that will happen in the two Title VII cases from this term, but this Congress doesn't seem to be able to move on anything," she said.

"In so many instances, the court and Congress have been having conversations with each other, particularly recently in the civil rights area," she said. "So it isn't good when you have a Congress that can't react."

The recent voting rights decision, Shelby County v. Holder, also invited Congress to enact new legislation. But Justice Ginsburg, who dissented, did not sound optimistic.

"The Voting Rights Act passed by overwhelming majorities," she said of its reauthorization in 2006, "but this Congress I don't think is equipped to do anything about it."

Asked if she was disappointed by the almost immediate tightening of voting laws in Texas and North Carolina after the decision, she chose a different word: "Disillusioned."

The flaw in the court's decision, she said, was to conclude from the nation's progress in protecting minority voters that the law was no longer needed. She repeated a line from her dissent: "It is like throwing away your umbrella in a rainstorm because you are not getting wet."

Chief Justice John G. Roberts Jr. wrote the majority opinion, and he quoted extensively from a 2009 decision that had, temporarily as it turned out, let the heart of the Voting Rights Act survive. Eight members of the court, including Justice Ginsburg, had signed the earlier decision.

On Friday, she said she did not regret her earlier vote, as the result in the 2009 case was correct. But she said she should have distanced herself from the majority opinion's language. "If you think it's going to do real damage, you don't sign on to it," she said. "I was mistaken in that case."

Some commentators have said that the two voting rights decisions are an example of the long game Chief Justice Roberts seems to be playing in several areas of the law, including campaign finance and affirmative action. Justice Ginsburg's lone dissent in June's affirmative action case, leaving in place the University of Texas' admissions plan but requiring lower courts to judge it against a more demanding standard, may suggest that she is alert to the chief justice's apparent strategy.

Justice Ginsburg is by her own description "this little tiny little woman," and she speaks in a murmur inflected with a Brooklyn accent. But she is a formidable force on the bench, often asking the first question at oral arguments in a way that frames the discussion that follows.

She has always been "a night person," she said, but she has worked even later into the small hours since her husband, Martin D. Ginsburg, a tax lawyer, chef and wit, died in 2010. Since then, she said, there is no one to call her to bed and turn out the lights.

She works out twice a week with a trainer and said her doctors at the National Institutes of Health say she is in fine health.

"Ever since my colorectal cancer in 1999, I have been followed by the N.I.H.," she said. "That was very lucky for me because they detected my pancreatic cancer at a very early stage" in 2009.

Less than three weeks after surgery for that second form of cancer, Justice Ginsburg was back on the bench.

"After the pancreatic cancer, at first I went to N.I.H. every three months, then every four months, then every six months," she said. "The last time I was there they said come back in a year."

Justice Ginsburg said her retirement calculations would center on her health and not on who would appoint her successor, even if that new justice could tilt the balance of the court and overturn some of the landmark women's rights decisions that are a large part of her legacy.

"I don't see that my majority opinions are going to be undone," she said. "I do hope that some of my dissents will one day be the law."

She said that as a general matter the court would be wise to move incrementally and methodically. It had moved too fast, she said, in Roe v. Wade, the 1973 decision that established a constitutional right to abortion. The court could have struck down only the extremely restrictive Texas law before it.

"I think it's inescapable that the court gave the anti-abortion forces a single target to aim at," she said. "The unelected judges decided this question for the country, and never mind that the issue was in flux in the state legislatures."

The question of same-sex marriage is also in flux around the nation. In June, the court declined to say whether there was a constitutional right to same-sex marriage, allowing the issue to percolate further. But Justice Ginsburg rejected the analogy to the lesson she had taken from the aftermath of the Roe decision.

"I wouldn't make a connection," she said.

The fireworks at the end of the last term included three dissents announced from the bench by Justice Ginsburg. Such oral dissents are rare and are reserved for major disagreements.

One was a sharp attack on Justice Samuel A. Alito Jr.'s majority opinion in a job discrimination case, and he made his displeasure known, rolling his eyes and making a face.

Justice Ginsburg said she took it in stride. "It was kind of a replay of the State of the Union, when he didn't agree with what the president was saying" in 2010 about the Citizens United decision. "It was his natural reaction, but probably if he could do it again, he would have squelched it."

Kagan Says Her Path to Supreme Court Was Made Smoother by Ginsburg's

BY ADAM LIPTAK | FEB. 10, 2014

THEY SHARE NEW YORK CITY ROOTS, a liberal outlook and a personal trainer. But a gap separates Justices Ruth Bader Ginsburg and Elena Kagan, one they explored during an often lighthearted joint appearance last week at the New York City Bar Association.

Justice Ginsburg, 80, is the oldest member of the Supreme Court, and she came of age when many legal careers were closed to women. Justice Kagan, 53, is the court's youngest member, and she seemed to have little trouble compiling a glittering résumé. She was the first female dean of Harvard Law School and the first female United States solicitor general.

"What explains this gulf between Justice Ginsburg's experience and mine?" Justice Kagan asked. "In large part the answer is simply Justice Ginsburg. As a litigator and then as a judge she changed the face of American antidiscrimination law."

Justice Ginsburg, having been turned down by law firms and refused judicial clerkships, became a professor at Rutgers Law School, where she experienced the sort of blatant discrimination that was common at the time. "Rutgers told her that she was going to be paid less than her male colleagues because, quote, your husband has a very good job," Justice Kagan said.

As a lawyer, Justice Ginsburg framed and argued cases that established an entirely new body of constitutional law, one requiring the equal treatment of women. As a judge, she kept pushing, sometimes in the face of headwinds from her more conservative colleagues.

In what Justice Kagan called "possibly the most effective dissent of this generation," Justice Ginsburg in 2007 called on Congress to overturn Ledbetter v. Goodyear Tire and Rubber Company, which said a federal law had imposed strict time limits for bringing lawsuits in workplace discrimination cases.

"I suspect that when Justice Ginsburg wrote those words she remembered her own experience of pay discrimination at Rutgers," Justice Kagan said.

Congress responded to the dissent with the Lilly Ledbetter Fair Pay Act of 2009. A framed copy of the law hangs in Justice Ginsburg's chambers.

The occasion for the justices' appearance last week was an annual lecture in Justice Ginsburg's honor, delivered this year by Justice Kagan. Justice Ginsburg introduced her colleague, saying her rise had been marked by wit and grit.

"The personal trainer with whom she boxes has been my physical fitness guardian since 1999," Justice Ginsburg said. "He tells me she has the best jab-cross-hook-punch combination on the federal bench."

Justice Kagan responded by taking a couple of affectionate jabs at the honoree. She admitted to having nursed a "minor grudge" for almost three decades arising from her efforts as a law student to secure a judicial clerkship on the United States Court of Appeals for the District of Columbia Circuit, where Justice Ginsburg served from 1980 to 1993 before joining the Supreme Court.

"I had the good fortune to be offered a clerkship by several of Justice Ginsburg's colleagues: Abner Mikva, whom I eventually clerked for, Harry Edwards and Pat Wald," Justice Kagan said. "The only one of President Carter's nominees to the D.C. Circuit who thought me not quite good enough was Judge Ginsburg. She didn't even interview me."

Justice Kagan also had a little fun with Justice Ginsburg's writing and interests. "As a law professor, she was a pathmarking scholar of civil procedure," Justice Kagan said, and then paused. "Pathmarking. Have you ever heard that word before? It appears in about 30 Justice Ginsburg opinions — although it appears actually not to exist. Oh well."

Justice Ginsburg is also an expert in comparative civil procedure, Justice Kagan said: "She wrote what I am confident is the definitive

American volume on civil procedure in Sweden. That's why when the Supreme Court faces a tricky question of Swedish civil procedure, we always go straight to Justice Ginsburg."

Justice Ginsburg later explained that the locution and her expertise in things Swedish were related. "Pathmarking" was a tribute, she said, to a book by the Swedish diplomat Dag Hammarskjold. (The book, a volume of journal entries, was called "Markings" in an English translation, though Swedes say "Waymarks" or "Pathmarks" would have been more apt.)

Justice Kagan, the newest justice, does not appear in public as often as some of her colleagues, but that is not saying much. The current Supreme Court ought to have its own speakers bureau. On the same day that Justices Ginsburg and Kagan appeared in New York, Justice Sonia Sotomayor was speaking in Connecticut, Justice Samuel A. Alito Jr. in Florida and Justice Antonin Scalia in Hawaii.

The two justices in New York had differing views about another sort of publicity: cameras at the Supreme Court. Justice Ginsburg was against them, on the ground that viewers would misunderstand the significance of oral arguments. The bulk of the court's work, she said, is based on written submissions and private discussion, reflection and writing.

"What the public will see is two people with a half-hour a side having a conversation with the justices, and they come away with the idea that, well, the best debater is going to win that contest," Justice Ginsburg said. "It would leave a false impression of the appellate process to think that the oral argument is what is decisive in the cases."

Justice Kagan was more equivocal. She acknowledged Justice Ginsburg's concern, along with the possibility of grandstanding, but she said there were important values on the other side.

"It's a really hard issue," she said. "Transparency is an important thing in government institutions, and for the most part the court would look pretty good."

On Justice Ginsburg's Summer Docket: Blunt Talk on Big Cases

BY ADAM LIPTAK | JULY 31, 2017

JUSTICE RUTH BADER GINSBURG is the most outspoken member of the Supreme Court, sometimes to her regret. Last year, she issued a statement saying that her criticisms of Donald J. Trump during the presidential campaign had been ill advised. "In the future," she said, "I will be more circumspect."

She has stayed true to her word, to a point, but she remains blunt and candid. In a pair of recent appearances, Justice Ginsburg critiqued the Trump administration's travel ban, previewed the coming court term, predicted an end to capital punishment and suggested that the other branches of government are in disarray.

Justice Ginsburg, 84, also described her grueling exercise routine, her link to a rap icon and her "graveyard" dissents.

The first appearance came two days after the Supreme Court issued a terse and cryptic unsigned order recalibrating how much of Mr. Trump's travel ban could be enforced while court challenges to it move forward. The order was two sentences long, and you could figure out what it meant mostly by inference.

The bottom line was a split decision: The administration could continue to bar many refugees but had to allow travel from six predominantly Muslim countries by grandparents and other relatives of United States residents.

Supreme Court justices typically let rulings in pending cases speak for themselves. Justice Ginsburg, delivering prepared remarks on July 21 at a Duke University School of Law event in Washington, explained what the court had meant in some detail. She made clear that she considered the recent order a rebuke to the Trump administration, saying its policy had been "too restrictive."

"Just this week, we clarified that closely related persons include grandparents," she said. "We decided that the government had been too restrictive in what family relationships qualify as close."

"The court also said," Justice Ginsburg continued, apparently referring to an earlier ruling, "that other people who could not be brought under the ban include students admitted to U.S. universities, a worker who has accepted employment from a U.S. company and a lecturer invited to address a U.S. audience. As to those individuals, the executive order may not be enforced pending our decision in the cases we will hear in October."

Justice Ginsburg discussed several other cases on the court's docket next term, including ones on the privacy of information held by cellphone companies, a clash between claims of religious freedom and same-sex marriage and a constitutional challenge to partisan gerrymandering.

That last case, Gill v. Whitford, No. 16-1161, could reshape American politics. Justice Ginsburg said the court's decision to hear the case was "perhaps the most important grant so far."

"So far, the court has held race-based gerrymandering unconstitutional but has not found a manageable, reliable measure of fairness for determining whether a partisan gerrymander violates the Constitution," she said.

In all, she said, "one can safely predict that next term will be a momentous one."

The court was shorthanded for much of the past two terms, from the death of Justice Antonin Scalia in February 2016 to the arrival of Justice Neil M. Gorsuch in April 2017.

The court mostly managed to avoid 4-to-4 deadlocks in the term that ended in June, rescheduling just two cases for reargument before a full court in the next term, starting in October. In general, Justice Ginsburg said, the justices try to achieve consensus, particularly in minor cases.

She said she will sometimes go along with the majority in, say, a tax case. "Even though I disagree, I will bury my dissent," she said. "We call that a graveyard dissent."

When the stakes are higher, she said, she takes a different approach.

"I will never compromise," she said, "when it's a question of, say, freedom of speech or press, gender equality."

A few days later, Justice Ginsburg spoke at George Washington University Law School, at an event sponsored by the Washington Council of Lawyers, a bar association.

Asked about the future of the death penalty in the United States, Justice Ginsburg did not mention a 2015 dissent in which she and Justice Stephen G. Breyer had called for a fresh look at the constitutionality of the practice. But she said capital punishment may soon be extinct in any event.

"The incidence of capital punishment has gone down, down, down so that now, I think, there are only three states that actually administer the death penalty," she said. "We may see an end to capital punishment by attrition as there are fewer and fewer executions."

The number of executions has indeed fallen sharply, with only 20 carried out in 2016, the smallest number in decades. But seven states have executed condemned inmates this year, according to the Death Penalty Information Center.

Her fans call her Notorious R.B.G., a nod to the rapper Notorious B.I.G., and Justice Ginsburg embraced the connection. "We were both born and bred in Brooklyn, New York," she said.

Justice Ginsburg said she works out with a personal trainer, completing squats, planks and push-ups while she watches public television. In October, her trainer, Bryant Johnson, will publish "The R.B.G. Workout: How She Stays Strong … and You Can Too!" It will include, the book's publisher said, "four-color illustrations of the justice in workout gear."

Justice Ginsburg did not mention Mr. Trump at either of her recent appearances, but she did say the Supreme Court enjoyed a more favorable reputation than the other parts of the federal government.

"If you took a poll today of the three branches of government, which one do the people think is doing the best job?" she asked. "We're way out in front of Congress."

She said nothing about the executive branch, or the man who leads it.

On Tour With Notorious R.B.G., Judicial Rock Star

BY ADAM LIPTAK | FEB. 8, 2018

THEY SAY THAT Bob Dylan, 76, is on a never-ending tour. Justice Ruth Bader Ginsburg, who is eight years older and has a day job, seems to have acquired Mr. Dylan's taste for the road.

In the space of three weeks, she is set to make at least nine public appearances. They follow a pattern: a thunderous standing ovation from an adoring crowd, followed by gentle questioning from a sympathetic interviewer.

Justice Ginsburg mixes familiar stories with insights about the Supreme Court and the law. She lands a couple of jokes. She promises not to step down so long as she can "do the job full steam." She describes her friendship with Justice Antonin Scalia, who died in 2016.

The audience swoons, and the show moves on to the next venue.

She seems to enjoy the attention. "I am soon to be 85," she said on Tuesday at New York Law School, "and everyone wants to take their picture with me."

Her fans call her Notorious R.B.G., a nod to the rapper Notorious B.I.G., and Justice Ginsburg embraces the connection. "We were both born and bred in Brooklyn, New York," she likes to say.

She was at the Sundance Film Festival in Utah on Jan. 21 for the premiere of a documentary on her career. The next day, she was absent from the Supreme Court bench, asking Chief Justice John G. Roberts Jr. to announce her majority opinion in a closely divided case in which she tangled with the court's newest member, Justice Neil M. Gorsuch.

Then it was on to Rhode Island for a "fireside chat" at a law school and an appearance before more than 1,000 people at a Providence synagogue. Those engagements caused her to miss President Trump's first State of the Union address. She had been a regular at President Obama's addresses.

Justice Ginsburg embracing Sheila Birnbaum, a lawyer, before taking the stage on Monday, where she recalled the years when she was the only woman on the court.

At the synagogue, Justice Ginsburg, who was sharply critical of Mr. Trump during the presidential campaign, said her talk had been planned before the date of his speech was announced.

"I'll say no more," she said. In response, a local reporter wrote, "the audience roared with knowing laughter."

On Monday, after an appearance last week at a Washington synagogue, Justice Ginsburg opened a three-day stand in New York City, speaking to 450 people at New York University's law school, with more watching from an overflow room. She spoke at a New York Law School luncheon on Tuesday and is scheduled to appear at Columbia University on Sunday.

The next day, she will be in Philadelphia, visiting both the National Constitution Center and the University of Pennsylvania.

Her New York appearances this week were studded with interesting remarks.

On Tuesday, for instance, she lamented the state of the Supreme Court confirmation process, recalling that Justice Scalia had been confirmed unanimously and that only three senators voted against her nomination.

"For the last four nominees, it hasn't been that way," she said, noting that there had been substantial partisan opposition to the nominations of Chief Justice John G. Roberts Jr. and Justices Samuel A. Alito Jr., Sonia Sotomayor and Elena Kagan. She did not mention Justice Gorsuch, who was confirmed by a vote of 54 to 45.

"My hope is that someday it will get back to the way it was," she said.

Her colleagues, she said, had offered extraordinary support during her two bouts with cancer. Justice David H. Souter, who avoided the Washington social scene before his retirement in 2009, accompanied her to the opera. Chief Justice William H. Rehnquist, who died in 2005, offered her a choice of majority opinions to write when she was facing chemotherapy.

"It never happened before," she said of the offer, "and it never happened since."

On Monday, Kenji Yoshino, a law professor at N.Y.U., asked about a recent study that showed that female justices are interrupted more often than male ones.

Justice Ginsburg said the article had gotten her attention. "Let's see how it affects my colleagues," she said. "I think it well may."

She recalled the years when she was the only woman on the court, between Justice Sandra Day O'Connor's retirement in 2006 and Justice Sotomayor's arrival in 2009. For those three years, she said, she shared the bench with "eight rather well-fed men."

Professor Yoshino reminded her that she had delivered a famous lecture at N.Y.U. not long before she joined the Supreme Court. The lecture criticized Roe v. Wade, the 1973 decision establishing a constitutional right to abortion.

The Supreme Court had moved too fast, Justice Ginsburg wrote at the time. It would have sufficed, she wrote, to strike down the extreme

Texas law at issue in the case and then proceeded in measured steps in later cases to consider other abortion restrictions.

The trend in state legislatures in the early 1970s, she wrote, was toward more liberal abortion laws. The categorical Roe decision, she wrote, gave rise to "a well-organized and vocal right-to-life movement" that "succeeded, for a considerable time, in turning the legislative tide in the opposite direction."

Her analysis is contested, as Justice Ginsburg acknowledged on Monday. "I know that there are many people who disagree with me on this subject," she said.

Nadine Strossen, a former president of the American Civil Liberties Union and a law professor at New York Law School, also asked about her critique of the Roe decision. Justice Ginsburg did not retreat but again said there were two sides to the question. "This is a highly debatable topic," she said.

Justice Ginsburg will celebrate her 25th anniversary on the court in August. She was appointed in 1993 by President Bill Clinton, who compared her work as a litigator for women's rights to Thurgood Marshall's work for racial equality.

The comparison was flawed, Justice Ginsburg said on Monday. "My life was never in danger," she said. "His was. He went to a southern town in the morning, and he couldn't be sure he'd be alive at the end of the day."

On Tuesday, she said she still relished her work, recalling a satisfying behind-the-scenes victory. "I can't disclose the opinion," she said, describing a dissent she had drafted after a tentative 7-to-2 vote. Her draft persuaded five colleagues to sign it, and she ended up writing for the majority in a 6-to-3 decision.

"So," Justice Ginsburg said, "it ain't over till it's over."

CHAPTER 3

Supreme Court Decisions

Ginsburg has heard and voted on hundreds of cases that have passed through the Supreme Court. As a self-professed night owl, she often stays up until 2 or 3 a.m., carefully crafting her decisions. While she has written majority opinions for many cases, she's also written her fair share of sharply worded dissents, particularly in the latter half of her tenure. These arguments have helped to inform the public and add a powerful voice to rulings spanning various hot-button issues such as reproductive rights, workplace discrimination and foreign policy.

In Her First Case, Ginsburg Dissents

BY LINDA GREENHOUSE | SEPT. 2, 1993

WASHINGTON, SEPT. 1 — In her first official act as a Supreme Court Justice, Ruth Bader Ginsburg was a dissenter today, joining two other members of the Court in voting to grant a stay of execution for a condemned Texas murderer who is scheduled to die on Friday.

A majority of six Justices voted to deny the stay in an unsigned order, with Justice Harry A. Blackmun and John Paul Stevens joining Justice Ginsburg in opposition. While Justice Ginsburg's vote did not affect the outcome, it provided the first indication that she may take a different approach to questions on the death penalty that did her predecessor, Justice Byron R. White.

Justice White rarely if ever voted to grant any of the numerous

Supreme Court Chief Justice William Rehnquist, right, swearing in new justice Ruth Bader Ginsburg last month as her husband Martin and President Bill Clinton, left, look on.

applications for stays of execution that reach the Court, and he was in the 5-to-4 majority in two cases last term in which the Court rejected constitutional challenges to the Texas death penalty statute. Lawyers for the inmate in today's case, Johnny James, raised a similar challenge to the Texas law and asked the Court to overrule the two recent decisions.

Because neither the majority nor the dissenters wrote opinions explaining their votes today, there was no way to know whether the Court considered the underlying issues or whether, by contrast, the application was rejected for essentially procedural reasons.

'A MORAL VICTORY'

Brent Newton, a lawyer with the Texas Resource Center in Houston who represented Mr. James, said he interpreted Justice Ginsburg's vote as an indication that she might be willing to reconsider the recent precedents that upheld the Texas law. "Getting her vote is a moral victory for us," Mr. Newton said.

Mr. James was sentenced to death for kidnapping and killing a woman in 1985. His conviction and sentence have been upheld by the Texas state courts and, most recently, by the United States Court of Appeals for the Fifth Circuit, in New Orleans, which rejected his petition for a writ of habeas corpus that challenged the constitutionality of his death sentence, as well as for a stay of execution.

An alcoholic who was drunk when he committed the crime, Mr. James argued that the Texas death penalty law unconstitutionally limited the jury's ability to evaluate his alcoholism as a factor that lessened his moral culpability and therefore argued against imposing a death sentence.

Four years ago, ruling in the case Penry v. Lynaugh, the Supreme Court found that the Texas law was constitutionally flawed because it did not permit a jury to give adequate weight to a capital defendant's mental retardation. The Texas law, which has since been amended, required the jury to decide whether a convicted murderer presented a future danger to society. In the Penry case, the Court found that this requirement made it more likely that a jury would weigh retardation as an argument for the death penalty rather than as a factor against it.

Military College Can't Bar Women, High Court Rules

BY LINDA GREENHOUSE | JUNE 27, 1996

WASHINGTON, JUNE 26 — The Supreme Court ruled today that under the "skeptical scrutiny" that applies to government action that treats men and women differently, the State of Virginia cannot justify keeping women out of its state-supported military college, the Virginia Military Institute.

"Women seeking and fit for a V.M.I.-quality education cannot be offered anything less under the state's obligation to afford them genuinely equal protection," Justice Ruth Bader Ginsburg said in a majority opinion for six Justices.

A seventh member of the Court, Chief Justice William H. Rehnquist, agreed in a separate opinion that the all-male admissions policy at the 157-year-old military college violated the Constitution and that the remedy accepted by the lower courts, a women's "leadership" program supported with state money at a nearby women's college, was inadequate.

The vote was therefore 7 to 1 on the basic constitutional holding in one of the Court's most important sex discrimination cases in years.

The lone dissenter was Justice Antonin Scalia, who objected that "change is forced upon Virginia, and reversion to single-sex education is prohibited nationwide, not by democratic processes but by order of this Court." Justice Clarence Thomas, whose son attends V.M.I., did not take part in the case.

The opinion leaves the state with the theoretical option of turning the college into a private institution, which would be free to exclude women. But officials at the school in Lexington, Va., indicated today that this option was probably not realistic.

"Whether or not it is feasible is very problematical," Maj. Gen. Josiah Bunting 3d, the superintendent of V.M.I., said at a news conference there this afternoon. "I must discourage speculation about that."

The board of trustees will meet July 12 and 13 and decide how to proceed, General Bunting said. A 1963 graduate of V.M.I., he described the ruling as a "savage disappointment."

Also at stake is the future of the Virginia Women's Institute for Leadership at Mary Baldwin College in Staunton, Va., where 42 students have just completed their first year of a program accepted by the lower courts as a valid alternative to admission to V.M.I.

Justice Ginsburg said that the women's program was only a "pale shadow" of what V.M.I. offered to male students and that it provided none of the considerable benefits of a degree from V.M.I., long one of the most prestigious educational institutions in the South. Chief Justice Rehnquist called the women's program "distinctly inferior."

General Bunting said a foundation supported by V.M.I. alumni would continue to provide financing for the Mary Baldwin program for four more years.

The country's only other state supported all-male college, The Citadel in South Carolina, will also be governed by the ruling today. South Carolina has also proposed a separate women's program at a private college, which is awaiting review in Federal District Court in Charleston.

The case presented the Court with two questions. The first was whether the exclusion of women violated the equal protection guarantee of the 14th Amendment, as the Justice Department charged when it sued the State of Virginia in Federal District Court in Roanoke in 1990. Once the Court found the all-male admissions policy to be unconstitutional, the second question was whether the alternative women's program was sufficient to remedy the violation.

The case had a complicated history in the lower courts, with the most recent ruling, a 1995 decision by the United States Court of Appeals for the Fourth Circuit, in Richmond, answering yes to both questions. The appeals court said that while the admissions policy deprived women of equal protection, the Mary Baldwin program was "sufficiently comparable" to a V.M.I. education to solve the problem.

For women actually to enroll at V.M.I. and take part in the rigorous military-style training there would destroy "any sense of decency that still permeates the relationship between the sexes," the appeals court said in an opinion that emphasized the spartan nature of barracks life and the brutalities of the "rat line" in which older students scream at and harass first-year cadets.

In her opinion today, Justice Ginsburg dismantled the appeals court's analysis in a manner both methodical and sweeping. While it might be true that most women would neither choose nor benefit from the educational methods at V.M.I., that was beside the point, she said, noting that the state never declared that a V.M.I. education was suitable for most men either.

"Generalizations about 'the way women are,' estimates of what is appropriate for most women, no longer justify denying opportunity to women whose talent and capacity place them outside the average description," Justice Ginsburg said. The state's alternative program "affords no cure at all for the opportunities and advantages withheld from women who want a V.M.I. education and can make the grade," she said.

Justice Ginsburg said Virginia's concern, as endorsed by the appeals court, that it would be destructive to place men and women together at V.M.I. reflected the same "ancient and familiar fear" that kept women out of law and other professions until well into modern times. She said the fact that women had graduated at the top of their classes from each of the Federal military academies and were serving successfully in the military indicated that "Virginia's fears for the future of V.M.I. may not be solidly grounded."

For Justice Ginsburg, a pioneer in the field of women's rights who as a private lawyer argued and won many of the Supreme Court precedents she cited in her opinion today, this was surely a moment of deep personal satisfaction.

There was a dramatic moment in her five-minute announcement when she began discussing a 1982 precedent, Mississippi University for Women v. Hogan — not one of her own cases — that held unconstitutional the exclusion of men from a state-supported nursing school. A state could not base admissions decisions on "archaic and stereotypic notions" of "proper" roles for men and women, the Hogan decision held.

The author of that decision was Justice Sandra Day O'Connor, then the junior Justice and still a curiosity as the first woman to serve on the Court. When Justice Ginsburg first referred to the Hogan case this morning, she lifted her eyes from the memo she was reading and gazed for a moment at Justice O'Connor. With just the barest hint of a smile, Justice O'Connor stared straight ahead.

The Clinton Administration had asked the Court to use this case, United States v. Virginia, No. 94-1941, to establish that official distinctions on the basis of sex should be just according to the same "strict scrutiny" that applies to distinctions based on race. The Court narrowly rejected taking that step in a case Justice Ginsburg argued in the 1970's.

Justice Ginsburg referred only obliquely to the issue today, instead applying what she called a "skeptical scrutiny" under which the state must demonstrate an "exceedingly persuasive justification" for any official action that treats men and women differently.

"The justification must be genuine, not hypothesized or invented post hoc in response to litigation," she said. "And it must not rely on overbroad generalizations about the different talents, capacities, or preferences of males and females."

She said that in its willingness to accept Virginia's alternative women's program as "sufficiently comparable," the appeals court ignored the Supreme Court's insistence on searching scrutiny in sex discrimination cases and "substituted a standard of its own invention."

The opinion today did not so much make new law on this issue as apply the existing standard in a forceful way. The Court's standard of review in sex discrimination cases "seemed to mean different things to different appeals courts" before today's decision, said Judith Lichtman, the president of the Women's Legal Defense Fund.

In his concurring opinion, Chief Justice Rehnquist objected that the Court had unnecessarily chosen a new verbal formulation, introducing an "element of uncertainty" into sex discrimination analysis.

The Chief Justice addressed Virginia's argument that an all-male V.M.I. served a policy of diversity in education. "The difficulty with its position is that the diversity benefited only one sex," the Chief Justice said, adding that while the Hogan decision "placed Virginia on notice" 14 years ago that the V.M.I. admissions policy was possibly unconstitutional, "the state did nothing." A high-quality, fully financed women's alternative program might have sufficed, he said.

In his dissenting opinion, which at 40 pages was a page shorter than the majority opinion, Justice Scalia described the decision as "not the interpretation of a Constitution, but the creation of one." He said that the rationale of the majority opinion threatened the continued existence of private single-sex colleges that receive various forms of Federal aid including tax-exempt status. But he said there was "substantial hope, I am happy and ashamed to say," that the Court would never take its analysis that far.

Cadets on the V.M.I. parade ground expressed deep disappointment today, saying the ruling would disturb the cohesion of the cadets.

"We don't have doors on the stalls in the bathrooms," said David F. Nash, a 20-year-old international studies major from Virginia Beach, who this fall will be a second-classman, or junior. "We have a group shower, and we have windows on our doors. There's virtually no place where you're really alone. It helps break you down. Everyone's equal: No one is behind a closed door, and no one is better."

Bush Prevails; By Single Vote, Justices End Recount, Blocking Gore After 5-Week Struggle

BY LINDA GREENHOUSE | DEC. 13, 2000

THE SUPREME COURT effectively handed the presidential election to George W. Bush tonight, overturning the Florida Supreme Court and ruling by a vote of 5 to 4 that there could be no further counting of Florida's disputed presidential votes.

The ruling came after a long and tense day of waiting at 10 p.m., just two hours before the Dec. 12 "safe harbor" for immunizing a state's electors from challenge in Congress was to come to an end. The unsigned majority opinion said it was the immediacy of this deadline that made it impossible to come up with a way of counting the votes that could both meet "minimal constitutional standards" and be accomplished within the deadline.

The five members of the majority were Chief Justice William H. Rehnquist and Justices Sandra Day O'Connor, Antonin Scalia, Anthony M. Kennedy and Clarence Thomas.

Among the four dissenters, two justices, Stephen G. Breyer and David H. Souter, agreed with the majority that the varying standards in different Florida counties for counting the punch-card ballots presented problems of both due process and equal protection. But unlike the majority, these justices said the answer should be not to shut the recount down, but to extend it until the Dec. 18 date for the meeting of the Electoral College.

Justice Souter said that such a recount would be a "tall order" but that "there is no justification for denying the state the opportunity to try to count all the disputed ballots now."

The six separate opinions, totaling 65 pages, were filled with evidence that the justices were acutely aware of the controversy the court had entered by accepting Governor Bush's appeal of last Friday's Florida Supreme Court ruling and by granting him a stay of the recount on Saturday afternoon, just hours after the vote counting had begun.

"None are more conscious of the vital limits on judicial authority than are the members of this court," the majority opinion said, referring to "our unsought responsibility to resolve the federal and constitutional issues the judicial system has been forced to confront."

The dissenters said nearly all the objections raised by Mr. Bush were insubstantial. The court should not have reviewed either this case or the one it decided last week, they said.

Justice John Paul Stevens said the court's action "can only lend credence to the most cynical appraisal of the work of judges throughout the land."

His dissenting opinion, also signed by Justices Breyer and Ruth Bader Ginsburg, added: "It is confidence in the men and women who administer the judicial system that is the true backbone of the rule of law. Time will one day heal the wound to that confidence that will be inflicted by today's decision. One thing, however, is certain. Although we may never know with complete certainty the identity of the winner of this year's Presidential election, the identity of the loser is perfectly clear. It is the nation's confidence in the judge as an impartial guardian of the rule of law."

What the court's day and a half of deliberations yielded tonight was a messy product that bore the earmarks of a failed attempt at a compromise solution that would have permitted the vote counting to continue.

It appeared that Justices Souter and Breyer, by taking seriously the equal protection concerns that Justices Kennedy and O'Connor had raised at the argument, had tried to persuade them that those concerns could be addressed in a remedy that would permit the disputed votes to be counted.

Justices O'Connor and Kennedy were the only justices whose names did not appear separately on any opinion, indicating that one or both of them wrote the court's unsigned majority opinion, labelled only "per curiam," or "by the court." Its focus was narrow, limited to the ballot counting process itself. The opinion objected not only to the varying standards used by different counties for determining voter intent, but to aspects of the Florida Supreme Court's order determining which ballots should be counted.

"We are presented with a situation where a state court with the power to assure uniformity has ordered a statewide recount with minimal procedural safeguards," the opinion said. "When a court orders a statewide remedy, there must be at least some assurance that the rudimentary requirements of equal treatment and fundamental fairness are satisfied."

Three members of the majority — the Chief Justice, and Justices Scalia and Thomas — raised further, more basic objections to the recount and said the Florida Supreme Court had violated state law in ordering it.

The fact that Justices O'Connor and Kennedy evidently did not share these deeper concerns had offered a potential basis for a coalition between them and the dissenters. That effort apparently foundered on the two justices' conviction that the midnight deadline of Dec. 12 had to be met.

The majority said that "substantial additional work" was needed to undertake a constitutional recount, including not only uniform statewide standards for determining a legal vote, but also "practical procedures to implement them" and "orderly judicial review of any disputed matters that might arise." There was no way all this could be done, the majority said.

The dissenters said the concern with Dec. 12 was misplaced. Justices Souter and Breyer offered to send the case back to the Florida courts "with instructions to establish uniform standards for evaluating the several types of ballots that have prompted differing treatments," as Justice Souter described his proposed remand order. He added: "unlike the majority, I see no warrant for this court to assume that Florida could not possibly comply with this requirement before the date set for the meeting of electors, Dec. 18."

Justices Stevens and Ginsburg said they did not share the view that the lack of a uniform vote-counting standard presented an equal protection problem.

In addition to joining Justice Souter's dissenting opinion, Justice Breyer wrote one of his own, signed by the three other dissenters, in which he recounted the history of the deadlocked presidential election of 1876 and of the partisan role that one Supreme Court justice, Joseph P. Bradley, played in awarding the presidency to Rutherford B. Hayes.

"This history may help to explain why I think it not only legally wrong, but also most unfortunate, for the Court simply to have terminated the Florida recount," Justice Breyer said. He said the time problem that Florida faced was "in significant part, a problem of the Court's own making." The recount was moving ahead in an "orderly fashion," Justice Breyer said, when "this court improvidently entered a stay." He said: "As a result, we will never know whether the recount could have been completed."

There was no need for the court to have involved itself in the election dispute this time, he said, adding: "Above all, in this highly politicized matter, the appearance of a split decision runs the risk of undermining the public's confidence in the court itself. That confidence is a public treasure. It has been built slowly over many years, some of which were marked by a Civil War and the tragedy of segregation. It is a vitally necessary ingredient of any successful effort to protect basic liberty and, indeed, the rule of law itself."

"We do risk a self-inflicted wound," Justice Breyer said, "a wound that may harm not just the court, but the nation."

Justice Ginsburg also wrote a dissenting opinion, joined by the other dissenters. Her focus was on the implications for federalism of the majority's action. "I might join the chief justice were it my commission to interpret Florida law," she said, adding: "The extraordinary setting of this case has obscured the ordinary principle that dictates its proper resolution: federal courts defer to state high courts' interpretations of their state's own law. This principle reflects the core of federalism, on which all agree."

"Were the other members of this court as mindful as they generally are of our system of dual sovereignty," Justice Ginsburg concluded, "they would affirm the judgment of the Florida Supreme Court."

Unlike the other dissenters, who said they dissented "respectfully," Justice Ginsburg said only: "I dissent."

Nothing about this case, Bush v. Gore, No. 00-949, was ordinary: not its context, not its acceptance over the weekend, not the enormously accelerated schedule with argument on Monday, and not the way the decision was released to the public tonight.

When the court issues an opinion, the justices ordinarily take the bench and the justice who has written for the majority gives a brief oral description of the case and the holding.

Today, after darkness fell and their work was done, the justices left the Supreme Court building individually from the underground garage, with no word to dozens of journalists from around the world who were waiting in the crowded pressroom for word as to when, or whether, a decision might come. By the time the pressroom staff passed out copies of the decision, the justices were gone.

Justice Ginsburg Backs Value of Foreign Law

BY ANNE E. KORNBLUT | APRIL 2, 2005

WASHINGTON, APRIL 1 — Justice Ruth Bader Ginsburg of the Supreme Court embraced the practice of consulting foreign legal decisions on Friday, rejecting the argument from conservatives that United States law should not take international thinking into account.

After a strongly worded dissent in a juvenile death penalty case from Justice Antonin Scalia last month that accused the court of putting too much faith in international opinion, Justice Ginsburg said the United States system should, if anything, consider international law more often.

"Judges in the United States are free to consult all manner of commentary," she said in a speech to several hundred lawyers and scholars here Friday.

She cited several instances when the logic of foreign courts had been applied to help untangle legal questions domestically, and of legislatures and courts abroad adopting United States law.

Fears about relying too heavily on world opinion "should not lead us to abandon the effort to learn what we can from the experience and good thinking foreign sources may convey," Justice Ginsburg told members of the American Society of International Law.

On March 1, the Supreme Court ruled 5 to 4 that the Constitution forbids executing convicts who committed their crimes before turning 18. The majority opinion reasoned that the United States was increasingly out of step with the world by allowing minors to be executed, saying "the United States now stands alone in a world that has turned its face against the juvenile death penalty."

Justice Scalia lambasted that logic, saying that "like-minded foreigners" should not be given a role in helping interpret the Constitution. House Republicans have introduced a resolution declaring that the "meaning of the Constitution of the United States should not be based on judgments, laws or pronouncements of foreign institutions unless such foreign judgments, laws or pronouncements inform an understanding of the original meaning of the Constitution of the United States."

In her speech, Justice Ginsburg criticized the resolutions in Congress and the spirit in which they were written. "Although I doubt the resolutions will pass this Congress, it is disquieting that they have attracted sizable support," she said.

"The notion that it is improper to look beyond the borders of the United States in grappling with hard questions has a certain kinship to the view that the U.S. Constitution is a document essentially frozen in time as of the date of its ratification," Justice Ginsburg said.

"Even more so today, the United States is subject to the scrutiny of a candid world," she said. "What the United States does, for good or for ill, continues to be watched by the international community, in particular by organizations concerned with the advancement of the rule of law and respect for human dignity."

Secretary of State Condoleezza Rice introduced Justice Ginsburg at the event, the first appearance by a sitting secretary of state before the 99-year-old organization in decades. Dr. Rice described Justice Ginsburg as "a great and good friend," adding that they also happened to be neighbors.

Justices' Ruling Limits Suits on Pay Disparity

BY LINDA GREENHOUSE | MAY 30, 2007

WASHINGTON, MAY 29 — The Supreme Court on Tuesday made it harder for many workers to sue their employers for discrimination in pay, insisting in a 5-to-4 decision on a tight time frame to file such cases. The dissenters said the ruling ignored workplace realities.

The decision came in a case involving a supervisor at a Goodyear Tire plant in Gadsden, Ala., the only woman among 16 men at the same management level, who was paid less than any of her colleagues, including those with less seniority. She learned that fact late in a career of nearly 20 years — too late, according to the Supreme Court's majority.

The court held on Tuesday that employees may not bring suit under the principal federal anti-discrimination law unless they have filed a formal complaint with a federal agency within 180 days after their pay was set. The timeline applies, according to the decision, even if the effects of the initial discriminatory act were not immediately apparent to the worker and even if they continue to the present day.

From 2001 to 2006, workers brought nearly 40,000 pay discrimination cases. Many such cases are likely to be barred by the court's interpretation of the requirement in Title VII of the Civil Rights Act of 1964 that employees make their charge within 180 days "after the alleged unlawful employment practice occurred."

Workplace experts said the ruling would have broad ramifications and would narrow the legal options of many employees.

In an opinion by Justice Samuel A. Alito Jr., the majority rejected the view of the federal agency, the Equal Employment Opportunity Commission, that each paycheck that reflects the initial discrimination is itself a discriminatory act that resets the clock on the 180-day period, under a rule known as "paycheck accrual."

"Current effects alone cannot breathe life into prior, uncharged discrimination," Justice Alito said in an opinion joined by Chief Justice John G. Roberts Jr. and Justices Antonin Scalia, Anthony M. Kennedy and Clarence Thomas. Justice Thomas once headed the employment commission, the chief enforcer of workers' rights under the statute at issue in this case, usually referred to simply as Title VII.

Under its longstanding interpretation of the statute, the commission actively supported the plaintiff, Lilly M. Ledbetter, in the lower courts. But after the Supreme Court agreed to hear the case last June, the Bush administration disavowed the agency's position and filed a brief on the side of the employer.

In a vigorous dissenting opinion that she read from the bench, Justice Ruth Bader Ginsburg said the majority opinion "overlooks common characteristics of pay discrimination." She said that given the secrecy in most workplaces about salaries, many employees would have no idea within 180 days that they had received a lower raise than others.

An initial disparity, even if known to the employee, might be small, Justice Ginsburg said, leading an employee, particularly a woman or a member of a minority group "trying to succeed in a nontraditional environment" to avoid "making waves." Justice Ginsburg noted that even a small differential "will expand exponentially over an employee's working life if raises are set as a percentage of prior pay."

Justices John Paul Stevens, David H. Souter and Stephen G. Breyer joined the dissent.

Ms. Ledbetter's salary was initially the same as that of her male colleagues. But over time, as she received smaller raises, a substantial disparity grew. By the time she brought suit in 1998, her salary fell short by as much as 40 percent; she was making $3,727 a month, while the lowest-paid man was making $4,286.

A jury in Federal District Court in Birmingham, Ala., awarded her more than $3 million in back pay and compensatory and punitive damages, which the trial judge reduced to $360,000. But the United States Court of Appeals for the 11th Circuit, in Atlanta, erased the verdict entirely, ruling that because Ms. Ledbetter could not show that she was the victim of intentional discrimination during the 180 days before she filed her complaint, she had not suffered an "unlawful employment practice" to which Title VII applied.

Several other federal appeals courts had accepted the employment commission's more relaxed view of the 180-day requirement. The justices accepted Ms. Ledbetter's appeal, Ledbetter v. Goodyear Tire and Rubber Company, No. 05-1074, to resolve the conflict.

Title VII's prohibition of workplace discrimination applies not just to pay but also to specific actions like refusal to hire or promote, denial of a desired transfer and dismissal. Justice Ginsburg argued in her dissenting opinion that while these "singular discrete acts" are readily apparent to an employee who can then make a timely complaint, pay discrimination often presents a more ambiguous picture. She said the court should treat a pay claim as it treated a claim for a "hostile work environment" in a 2002 decision, permitting a charge to be filed "based on the cumulative effect of individual acts."

In response, Justice Alito dismissed this as a "policy argument" with "no support in the statute."

As with an abortion ruling last month, this decision showed the impact of Justice Alito's presence on the court. Justice Sandra Day O'Connor, whom he succeeded, would almost certainly have voted the other way, bringing the opposite outcome.

The impact of the decision on women may be somewhat limited by the availability of another federal law against sex discrimination in the workplace, the Equal Pay Act, which does not contain the 180-day requirement. Ms. Ledbetter initially included an Equal Pay Act complaint, but did not pursue it. That law has additional procedural hurdles and a low damage cap that excludes punitive damages. It does not cover discrimination on the basis of race or Title VII's other protected categories.

In her opinion, Justice Ginsburg invited Congress to overturn the decision, as it did 15 years ago with a series of Supreme Court rulings on civil rights. "Once again, the ball is in Congress's court," she said. Within hours, Senator Hillary Rodham Clinton of New York, who is seeking the Democratic nomination, announced her intention to submit such a bill.

Oral Dissents Give
Ginsburg a New Voice on Court

BY LINDA GREENHOUSE | MAY 31, 2007

WASHINGTON, MAY 30 — Whatever else may be said about the Supreme Court's current term, which ends in about a month, it will be remembered as the time when Justice Ruth Bader Ginsburg found her voice, and used it.

Both in the abortion case the court decided last month and the discrimination ruling it issued on Tuesday, Justice Ginsburg read forceful dissents from the bench. In each case, she spoke not only for herself but also for three other dissenting colleagues, Justices John Paul Stevens, David H. Souter and Stephen G. Breyer.

But the words were clearly her own, and they were both passionate and pointed. In the abortion case, in which the court upheld the federal Partial-Birth Abortion Ban Act seven years after having struck down a similar state law, she noted that the court was now "differently composed than it was when we last considered a restrictive abortion regulation." In the latest case, she summoned Congress to overturn what she called the majority's "parsimonious reading" of the federal law against discrimination in the workplace.

To read a dissent aloud is an act of theater that justices use to convey their view that the majority is not only mistaken, but profoundly wrong. It happens just a handful of times a year. Justice Antonin Scalia has used the technique to powerful effect, as has Justice Stevens, in a decidedly more low-key manner.

The oral dissent has not been, until now, Justice Ginsburg's style. She has gone years without delivering one, and never before in her 15 years on the court has she delivered two in one term. In her past dissents, both oral and written, she has been reluctant to breach the court's collegial norms. "What she is saying is that this is not law, it's politics," Pamela S. Karlan, a Stanford law professor, said of Justice

Ginsburg's comment linking the outcome in the abortion case to the fact of the court's changed membership. "She is accusing the other side of making political claims, not legal claims."

The justice's acquaintances have watched with great interest what some depict as a late-career transformation. "Her style has always been very ameliorative, very conscious of etiquette," said Cynthia Fuchs Epstein, the sociologist and a longtime friend. "She has always been regarded as sort of a white-glove person, and she's achieved a lot that way. Now she is seeing that basic issues she's fought so hard for are in jeopardy, and she is less bound by what have been the conventions of the court."

Some might say her dissents are an expression of sour grapes over being in the minority more often than not. But there may be strategic judgment, as well as frustration, behind Justice Ginsburg's new style. She may have concluded that quiet collegiality has proved futile and that her new colleagues, Chief Justice John G. Roberts Jr. and Justice Samuel A. Alito Jr., are not open to persuasion on the issues that matter most to her.

Justice Alito, of course, took the place of Justice Sandra Day O'Connor, with whom Justice Ginsburg formed a deep emotional bond, although they differed on a variety of issues. And Chief Justice Roberts succeeded Chief Justice William H. Rehnquist, with whom Justice Ginsburg often disagreed but maintained a relationship that was at times surprisingly productive.

For example, in 1996, over Justice Scalia's vigorous dissent, the chief justice gave Justice Ginsburg his vote in a decision holding that the Virginia Military Institute's men-only admissions policy was unconstitutional. In 2003, they made common cause in a case that strengthened the Family and Medical Leave Act. When Justice Ginsburg criticized a Rehnquist opinion, she did so gently; today's adversary could be tomorrow's ally.

If there has been any such meeting of the minds between Justice Ginsburg and her new colleagues, it has not been evident. She may have concluded that her side's interests are better served by appealing not to the court's majority but to the public. "She's sounding an alarm and wants people to take notice," said Debra L. Ness, president of the National Partnership for Women and Families, an advocacy group that focuses on the workplace.

Goodwin Liu, a law professor at the University of California, Berkeley, was one of Justice Ginsburg's law clerks when the court decided the 2000 election case, the bitterly divided Bush v. Gore decision, from which she dissented. Even during that freighted period, Professor Liu said, "I was struck by how much of an institutional citizen she was, how attuned to the wishes of her colleagues and to not giving offense."

Professor Liu said that when he read the dissent on Tuesday, it occurred to him that in recounting the workplace travails of the plaintiff, Lilly M. Ledbetter, Justice Ginsburg was also telling a version of her own story. "Here she is, the one woman of a nine-member body, describing the get-along imperative and the desire not to make waves felt by the one woman among 16 men," Professor Liu said. "It's as if after 15 years on the court, she's finally voicing some complaints of her own."

Another of the justice's friends, Prof. Judith Resnik of Yale Law School, noted that throughout her legal career, Justice Ginsburg has been deeply concerned about questions of access to the courts and the remedial powers of federal judges, themes she has explored in both majority and dissenting opinions. "Those of us reading not just the grand-slam cases but the quieter ones have heard her voice," Professor Resnik said. She added, "Now that the stakes are going up, more people will be listening."

Supreme Court Raises Bar
to Prove Job Discrimination

BY STEVEN GREENHOUSE | JUNE 24, 2013

IN TWO DECISIONS ISSUED on Monday, the Supreme Court effectively made it harder for workers to prove that they had suffered employment discrimination.

One ruling narrows the definition of what constitutes a supervisor in racial and sexual harassment cases, while the other adopts a tougher standard for workers to prove that they had faced illegal retaliation for complaining about employment discrimination.

In both cases, the rulings were decided by a 5-to-4 majority, with the dissenting justices, the court's four most liberal members, calling on Congress to fix what they said were overly restrictive rulings.

In Vance v. Ball State University, in which an African-American worker accused her supervisor of racial harassment, the court held that the person she accused was a co-worker and not a supervisor — a distinction that requires a higher burden of proof for the plaintiff's employer to be found liable.

The majority decision, written by Justice Samuel A. Alito Jr., rejected the definition of "supervisor" advanced by the Equal Employment Opportunity Commission as someone authorized to take "tangible employment actions" or direct the employee's daily work activities.

Rather, the court ruled that being a supervisor should be limited to someone authorized to take "tangible employment actions" like hiring, firing, promoting, demoting or reassigning employees to significantly different responsibilities.

Justice Alito, noting that there are numerous definitions of who is a supervisor, wrote that "the ability to direct another employee's tasks is simply not sufficient" to declare someone a supervisor. He ridiculed the E.E.O.C's definition of supervisor, saying it was a "study in ambiguity."

The plaintiff, Maetta Vance, a banquet worker at Ball State University in Muncie, Ind., asserted that Saundra Davis, who is white and was described as a catering specialist, had glared at her, slammed pots and pans around her and blocked her on an elevator. Both sides agreed that Ms. Davis did not have the authority to hire or fire employees.

Under previous Supreme Court decisions, plaintiffs claiming racial or sexual harassment faced a lower burden to prove an employer liable when the harassment was committed by a supervisor rather than a co-worker. For instance, if the harassing supervisor was found to have taken adverse actions against an employee, like demoting the person, the employer was strictly liable for that action. And even when a supervisor's harassment did not culminate in a specific negative employment action, the employer could be held liable if the employer failed to prove that it exercised reasonable care to prevent and correct any harassing behavior.

But for an employer to be held liable when a co-worker is accused of harassment, the plaintiff has the burden of proving that the employer was negligent by not stopping the behavior.

The court upheld a decision by the Seventh Circuit Court of Appeals that held that Ms. Davis was not a supervisor and that Ball State was not negligent with respect to her behavior. Justice Alito emphasized that the court's adoption of a narrower definition of supervisor did not leave plaintiffs unprotected, but left them with a different burden of proof.

In a stinging dissent, Justice Ruth Bader Ginsburg argued that the majority opinion "is blind to the realities of the workplace." She wrote that it is not easy for an employee to tell a harassing supervisor to "buzz off" even when the supervisor does not have the power to fire or demote.

"An employee who confronts her harassing supervisor risks, for example, receiving an undesirable or unsafe work assignment or an unwanted transfer," Justice Ginsburg wrote. "She may be saddled with an excessive workload" or a shift that disrupts her family life.

Asserting that the ruling undermines Congress's desire for "robust protection against workplace discrimination," Justice Ginsburg warned that the decision would relieve employers of responsibility for the behavior of many of their supervisors.

"The ball is once again in Congress' court to correct the error into which this Court has fallen," she wrote.

In a second employment decision issued on Monday, University of Texas Southwestern Medical Center v. Nassar, the court tightened the legal standard for plaintiffs who assert that they faced adverse employment actions in retaliation for complaining about employment discrimination. The court held that the plaintiff must prove that the retaliation was not just a motivating factor in a negative action like a demotion but the determinative factor.

The majority decision, written by Justice Anthony M. Kennedy, engaged in lengthy textual interpretation of Title VII of the Civil Rights Act. Justice Kennedy said retaliation cases should have a different, tougher standard of proof than in regular employment discrimination cases under the act. In typical discrimination cases, employers can be held liable if wrongful discrimination is a motivating factor.

The case involved Naiel Nassar, a physician of Middle Eastern descent, who claimed that he faced hostile treatment from a hospital superior because of his religion and ethnic heritage. He further claimed that he had been retaliated against — that he was not given as good a job offer as he had hoped — because he had complained of discrimination.

Justice Kennedy said it was important to have the proper causation standard in retaliation cases because the number of such cases filed with the E.E.O.C. has nearly doubled in the last 15 years, rising to more than 31,000 in 2012. The court vacated the Fifth Circuit's ruling and remanded the case for further proceedings.

Writing the dissent, Justice Ginsburg said the tougher "but-for causation standard" that the court was adopting for retaliation cases would undercut efforts to fight employment discrimination. She also warned that juries would be confused in hearing cases in which employment discrimination claims would be judged by one standard and related retaliation claims by a tougher standard.

Justice Ruth Bader Ginsburg wrote the minority opinion in one case.

Justice Ginsburg concluded that Monday's two employment-related decisions "should prompt yet another Civil Rights Restoration Act," a 1987 law that in effect overturned several Supreme Court rulings.

Supreme Court Bars Favoring Mothers Over Fathers in Citizenship Case

BY ADAM LIPTAK | JUNE 12, 2017

WASHINGTON — Unwed mothers and fathers may not be treated differently in determining whether their children may claim American citizenship, the Supreme Court ruled on Monday. "The gender line Congress drew is incompatible with the requirement that the government accord to all persons 'the equal protection of the laws,' " Justice Ruth Bader Ginsburg wrote for the majority.

The case concerned Luis Ramon Morales-Santana, who was born in 1962 in the Dominican Republic. His father was an American citizen, but his mother was not. His parents were unwed but later married.

The family moved to the United States when Mr. Morales-Santana was 13, and he lived in this country for decades. After convictions for robbery, attempted murder and other crimes, federal authorities sought to deport him.

He resisted, claiming American citizenship. But the law in effect when he was born allowed unwed fathers of children born abroad to transmit citizenship to them only if the fathers had lived in the United States before the child was born for a total of 10 years, five of them after age 14. Mr. Morales-Santana's father fell just short of satisfying that requirement.

The same law made it much easier for unwed mothers to transmit citizenship to their children, requiring them to have lived in the United States for a year before their child was born. (The law has since been amended, but it continues to favor mothers over fathers.)

The United States Court of Appeals for the Second Circuit, in New York, ruled for Mr. Morales-Santana, saying that the differing treatment of mothers and fathers was unconstitutional sex discrimination. The appeals court declared him a citizen.

Justice Ginsburg agreed that the law was based on stereotypes that violated equal protection principles. The law, she wrote, was built on a faulty assumption "that unwed fathers care little about, indeed are strangers to, their children."

"Lump characterization of that kind, however, no longer passes equal protection inspection," Justice Ginsburg wrote.

Chief Justice John G. Roberts Jr. and Justices Anthony M. Kennedy, Stephen G. Breyer, Sonia Sotomayor and Elena Kagan joined the majority opinion in the case, Sessions v. Morales-Santana, No. 15-1191.

Justice Ginsburg said treating mothers and fathers differently was unjustified.

"The scheme permits the transmission of citizenship to children who have no tie to the United States so long as their mother was a U.S. citizen continuously present in the United States for one year at any point in her life prior to the child's birth," she wrote. "The transmission holds even if the mother marries the child's alien father immediately after the child's birth and never returns with the child to the United States.

"At the same time," Justice Ginsburg wrote, "the legislation precludes citizenship transmission by a U.S.-citizen father who falls a few days short of meeting" the law's "longer physical-presence requirements, even if the father acknowledges paternity on the day of the child's birth and raises the child in the United States."

Having decided that mothers and fathers must be treated the same, Justice Ginsburg delivered some bad news to Mr. Morales-Santana. Ordinarily, she wrote, the court would extend the benefits conferred by the statute to the disfavored group. In this case, that would mean allowing Mr. Morales-Santana the benefit of the one-year period.

But the shorter period for unwed mothers, she wrote, was an exception to a general rule, one that also applied to married parents. The right solution, she wrote, was to subject all children seeking citizenship under the statute to the longer period.

"Going forward," Justice Ginsburg wrote, "Congress may address the issue and settle on a uniform prescription that neither favors nor disadvantages any person on the basis of gender."

In the meantime, she added, the law's "now-five-year requirement should apply, prospectively, to children born to unwed U.S.-citizen mothers."

Mr. Morales-Santana will now be subject to deportation proceedings.

In a concurrence, Justice Clarence Thomas, joined by Justice Samuel A. Alito Jr., wrote that the court had decided more than it had to. Since it was powerless to grant relief to Mr. Morales-Santana, Justice Thomas wrote, it was unnecessary to decide whether the law violated equal protection principles.

In a second decision on Monday, Henson v. Santander Consumer USA, No. 16-349, Justice Neil M. Gorsuch issued his first opinion. Writing for a unanimous court, he said it was for Congress rather than the court to address a possible gap in a federal debt collection law.

When Congress enacted the Fair Debt Collection Practices Act in 1977, it imposed strict regulations on firms that collected other companies' debts. But it did not address the activities of businesses like banks, credit card companies and car dealerships that collect their own debts.

That distinction failed to anticipate an increasingly popular business model, in which companies buy distressed debt outright and then try to collect it. The question in the case was whether such companies qualified as debt collectors under the law.

"Everyone agrees that the term embraces the repo man — someone hired by a creditor to collect an outstanding debt," Justice Gorsuch wrote. "But what if you purchase a debt and then try to collect it for yourself — does that make you a 'debt collector' too? That's the nub of the dispute now before us."

He concluded that the law as written did not reach the new business model.

"While it is of course our job to apply faithfully the law Congress has written," Justice Gorsuch wrote, "it is never our job to rewrite a constitutionally valid statutory text under the banner of speculation about what Congress might have done had it faced a question that, on everyone's account, it never faced."

Justice Ginsburg and the Price of Equality

OPINION | BY LINDA GREENHOUSE | JUNE 22, 2017

THE FLOOD OF NEWS in recent days has all but swamped a fascinating Supreme Court decision that deserves more than a footnote to the term now coming to an end. The ruling defied expectations in nearly every way that counted and suggests a more complex picture of the Roberts court than its notably ideology-riven decisions usually offer.

The subject was citizenship, specifically the circumstances under which children born overseas to unmarried parents acquire United States citizenship when one parent is a citizen and the other isn't. Cases dealing with citizenship have often sharply divided the court; in fact, six years ago, with Justice Elena Kagan recused, a four to four tie left the justices unable to resolve the precise question the court decided last week in Sessions v. Morales-Santana with near unanimity.

The justices typically defer to Congress in cases concerning citizenship. But this time, the court declared unconstitutional a provision of the Immigration and Nationality Act that makes the path to citizenship for foreign-born children of unmarried parents dependent on whether the citizen-parent is the mother or the father. An unwed mother can transmit her citizenship as long as she herself has lived in the United States for at least one year. But for unwed fathers, the prebirth residency requirement is five years (it was 10 years before a 1986 amendment). The differential treatment of mothers and fathers, six justices held in an opinion by Justice Ruth Bader Ginsburg, violates the constitutional guarantee of equal protection.

Justice Ginsburg's distinctive voice was evident throughout the opinion, which drew on the sex discrimination cases she argued and won before the Supreme Court as a young advocate for women's rights (many of those cases, like this one, had male plaintiffs) as well as on a landmark majority opinion she delivered early in her Supreme Court tenure that forced the all-male Virginia Military Institute to admit women. The greater burden placed on unwed fathers, she wrote in the new case, reflected age-old assumptions about unmarried parenthood and a stereotyped view of an unwed father's ability to be a responsible parent: "Overbroad generalizations of that order, the court has come to comprehend, have a constraining impact, descriptive though they may be of the way many people still order their lives." The law's distinction between men and women, she wrote, "is stunningly anachronistic."

It was pure Ginsburg. The justice noted that the immigration law's basic framework dates from the 1940s and '50s, "an era when the law-books of our nation were rife with overbroad generalizations about the way men and women are." Are what? Just "are." At the core of Ruth Ginsburg's lifelong project is the conviction that there should be no separate spheres for men and women in the eyes of the law, and that distinctions based on what "most" men or women do, on the choices that "most" of them make, is an obstacle to full legal equality.

DOUG MILLS/THE NEW YORK TIMES

Justice Ruth Bader Ginsburg, seated far left, with her fellow Supreme Court justices this month.

Anyone acquainted with Justice Ginsburg's body of work would have found many familiar passages in her majority opinion. But then at the end came the decision's stunner. Although Luis Ramon Morales-Santana, the Dominican-born man who brought the case — and whose United States citizen father failed by just 20 days to meet the 10-year residency requirement that was in effect when Luis was born — won his constitutional argument, his victory was a hollow one. Striking down the mother-father distinction did not, at the end of the day, make him a citizen. In fact, because of a criminal record, he now faces deportation to the Dominican Republic, which he left at age 13, 41 years ago.

When a court decides that a law violates the equal protection guarantee by treating differently two classes of people who should be treated the same, it has two choices: confer the benefit on both groups, or take it away from the class the law favored. In either event, the two groups end up being treated the same, and equal protection is served. Nearly always, the Supreme Court has chosen to "level up" — to confer the benefit on both. This was the result in the cases the young Ruth Ginsburg won. Federal benefits to families with dependent children, specified in the Social Security Act as available only to families with unemployed fathers, were extended to families with unemployed mothers. And Social Security benefits available only to widows were extended to widowers.

But in this case, the court leveled not up, but down. Congress itself should fix the problem, Justice Ginsburg wrote, but until it does — an optimistic "in the interim" — the five-year residency requirement for unmarried fathers will now apply to unmarried mothers as well. (Justice Ginsburg made clear that the change was prospective only.) This outcome raises the question: What, then, was the point of this case? Some untold number of children, to be born in the future, outside the country's borders, to unmarried American citizen mothers, will undoubtedly be worse off than they would have been had the challenge to the mother-father distinction never come before the Supreme Court in the first place. Formal equality was achieved, to be sure, but it was equality with a price — a high price for many.

In her opinion, Justice Ginsburg addressed why "this court is not equipped to grant the relief Morales-Santana seeks." She explained that the general rule set by Congress for conveying citizenship to foreign-born children when the parents are married subjects citizen fathers and mothers to the longer residency requirement. The shorter requirement for unwed citizen mothers is itself an exception to the general rule.

The question for the court, she continued, was what choice Congress would have made had it known that the exception was constitutionally vulnerable: Would it have extended the exception to unwed fathers, or would it have withheld it from the mothers? "Although extension of benefits is customary in federal benefit cases," she wrote, "all indicators in this case point in the opposite direction. Put to the choice, Congress, we believe, would have abrogated [the] exception, preferring preservation of the general rule."

Was this explanation persuasive? Not to me, actually, but then I wasn't Justice Ginsburg's primary audience. Her fellow justices were. When the case was argued last Nov. 9, it was clear that the court was going to struggle with the question of remedy if it found an equal protection violation. And the more than seven months that elapsed from argument to decision made it clear that a struggle was going on. By the time of the June 12 decision, the case was the oldest undecided case on the court's calendar. (By contrast, two of the cases the court decided on Monday of this week were argued in late April.)

Justice Ginsburg is one of the fastest writers on the court, so obviously some heavy negotiating was going on during those seven months. Was leveling down the price she had to pay to hold a majority? Two justices, Clarence Thomas and Samuel A. Alito Jr., wrote separately that they agreed with the remedy, thus providing a unanimous 8-0 vote for the final judgment. (Justice Neil Gorsuch didn't have a vote, since he joined the court after the case was argued.) The two justices added in their two-paragraph opinion that because "the court's remedial holding resolves this case," there was no need to have decided the constitutional issue.

The fact that Chief Justice John G. Roberts Jr. joined Justice Ginsburg's opinion in full is intriguing. Finding an equal protection violation doesn't come naturally to him. In fact, he almost certainly voted to uphold the mother-father distinction in Flores-Villar v. United States, the case that ended in a tie vote (and therefore without an opinion) six years ago. Assuming that Justices Stephen G. Breyer, Anthony M. Kennedy and Sonia Sotomayor joined Justice Ginsburg then in voting to strike down the distinction, Chief Justice Roberts must have voted with Justices Thomas, Alito and Antonin Scalia to uphold it. Something persuaded him to change his mind. Maybe the remedial judgment gave him sufficient comfort.

And what about Justice Ginsburg? Can we assume she's happy with the outcome of the case, or do we suppose she wrote the remedial section with gritted teeth? Twenty-four years ago, in July 1993, she was President Bill Clinton's first Supreme Court nominee, and I covered her Senate confirmation hearing. I had met Judge Ginsburg several times, but didn't know her well. I found her Judiciary Committee testimony enlightening, and I wrote an analysis that appeared under the headline "A Sense of Judicial Limits." I described her as "something of a rare creature in the modern judicial lexicon: a judicial restraint liberal." By that I meant that while her own commitments were to liberal outcomes, she displayed an equally strong commitment to letting Congress take the lead. "In her view, equality — or any other goal — is best achieved if all branches of government have a stake in achieving it."

So I'm ready to assume that if the remedial portion of her opinion last week was a compromise, it was one she offered willingly. Her "over to you, Congress" handoff may seem naïve in the present political climate, but it conforms with her deepest beliefs about the appropriate judicial role.

And it's worth remembering that from her earliest years as a nervous young lawyer standing before the nine men of the Supreme Court, Ruth Ginsburg has always played a long game, with the ultimate goal, equality of the sexes, constantly in view. As this case turned out, the price for equality was high. But I don't doubt that for Justice Ginsburg, it was a price worth paying for being able to strike a blow against still another law based on a generalization about the way "men and women are."

LINDA GREENHOUSE is a Pulitzer Prize-winning reporter for The New York Times covering the Supreme Court and the law.

Supreme Court Upholds Workplace Arbitration Contracts Barring Class Actions

BY ADAM LIPTAK | MAY 21, 2018

WASHINGTON — The Supreme Court on Monday ruled that companies can use arbitration clauses in employment contracts to prohibit workers from banding together to take legal action over workplace issues.

The vote was 5 to 4, with the court's more conservative justices in the majority. The court's decision could affect some 25 million employment contracts.

Writing for the majority, Justice Neil M. Gorsuch said the court's conclusion was dictated by a federal law favoring arbitration and the court's precedents. If workers were allowed to band together to press their claims, he wrote, "the virtues Congress originally saw in arbitration, its speed and simplicity and inexpensiveness, would be shorn away and arbitration would wind up looking like the litigation it was meant to displace."

Justice Ruth Bader Ginsburg read her dissent from the bench, a sign of profound disagreement. In her written dissent, she called the majority opinion "egregiously wrong." In her oral statement, she said the upshot of the decision "will be huge under-enforcement of federal and state statutes designed to advance the well being of vulnerable workers."

Justice Ginsburg called on Congress to address the matter.

Brian T. Fitzpatrick, a law professor at Vanderbilt University who studies arbitrations and class actions, said the ruling was unsurprising in light of earlier Supreme Court decisions. Justice Gorsuch, he added, "appears to have put his cards on the table as firmly in favor of allowing class actions to be stamped out through arbitration agreements."

As a result, Professor Fitzpatrick said "it is only a matter of time until the most powerful device to hold corporations accountable for their misdeeds is lost altogether."

But Gregory F. Jacob, a lawyer with O'Melveny & Myers in Washington, said the decision would have a limited impact, as many employers already use the contested arbitration clauses. "This decision thus will not see a huge increase in the use of such provisions," he said, "but it does protect employers' settled expectations and avoids placing our nation's job providers under the threat of additional burdensome litigation drain."

Justice Gorsuch wrote that there are policy arguments on both sides of the dispute but that the role of the courts was to interpret the governing statutes.

"The respective merits of class actions and private arbitration as means of enforcing the law are questions constitutionally entrusted not to the courts to decide but to the policymakers in the political branches where those questions remain hotly contested," he wrote.

Chief Justice John G. Roberts Jr. and Justices Anthony M. Kennedy, Clarence Thomas and Samuel A. Alito Jr. joined the majority opinion.

The cases featured an unusual element: Lawyers for the federal government appeared on both sides.

The Obama administration had filed a brief supporting the workers on behalf of the National Labor Relations Board. The Trump administration reversed course, and it argued on behalf of the employers. The labor board's general counsel, however, argued for the workers.

The three consolidated cases decided Monday concerned charges that employers had underpaid their workers. The workers' employment contracts required that they resolve such disputes in arbitration rather than court and, importantly, that they file their claims one by one.

Arbitration clauses in employment contracts are a recent innovation, but they have become quite common. In 1992, Justice Ginsburg wrote, only 2 percent of non-unionized employers used mandatory arbitration agreements, while 54 percent do so today. Some 23 percent of employees not represented by unions, she wrote, are subject to employment contracts that require class-action waivers.

Under those contracts, Justice Ginsburg wrote, it is often not worth it and potentially dangerous to pursue small claims individually. "By joining hands in litigation, workers can spread the costs of litigation and reduce the risk of employer retaliation," she wrote.

The contracts may also encourage misconduct, Justice Ginsburg wrote.

"Employers, aware that employees will be disinclined to pursue small-value claims when confined to proceeding one-by-one, will no doubt perceive that the cost-benefit balance of underpaying workers tips heavily in favor of skirting legal obligations," she wrote, adding that billions of dollars in underpaid wages are at issue.

Justice Ginsburg added that requiring individual arbitrations can produce inconsistent results in similar cases, particularly because arbitrations are often confidential.

Justices Stephen G. Breyer, Sonia Sotomayor and Elena Kagan joined Justice Ginsburg's dissent.

In response, Justice Gorsuch wrote that Justice Ginsburg was overstating things. "Like most apocalyptic warnings, this one is a false alarm," he wrote. "Our decision does nothing to override Congress's policy judgments."

The case was the court's latest attempt to determine how far companies can go in insisting that disputes be resolved in individual arbitrations rather than in court.

The Supreme Court ruled in earlier cases that companies doing business with consumers may require arbitration and forbid class actions in their contracts, which are often of the take-it-or-leave-it variety.

The question for the justices in the new cases is whether the same principles apply to employment contracts.

In both settings, the challenged contracts require that disputes be raised through the informal mechanism of arbitration rather than in court and that claims be brought one by one. That makes it hard to pursue minor claims that affect many people, whether in class actions or in mass arbitrations.

In 2011, in AT&T Mobility v. Concepcion, the Supreme Court ruled that the Federal Arbitration Act, which favors arbitration, allowed companies to avoid class actions by insisting on individual arbitrations in their contracts with consumers.

By a 5-to-4 vote, the court said a California couple who objected to a $30 charge for what had been advertised as a free cellphone were barred from banding together with other unhappy customers.

Arbitration clauses with class waivers are now commonplace in contracts for things like cellphones, credit cards, rental cars and nursing home care.

In a 2015 dissent, Justice Ginsburg, citing a New York Times article examining arbitration agreements, wrote that the 2011 decision and later ones "have predictably resulted in the deprivation of consumers' rights to seek redress for losses, and, turning the coin, they have insulated powerful economic interests from liability for violations of consumer protection laws."

In the cases decided Monday, workers argued that employment contracts are different. They said a second law, the National Labor Relations Act, prohibits class waivers. The labor law protects workers' rights to engage in "concerted activities."

Two federal appeals courts, in Chicago and San Francisco, accepted that argument. A third, in New Orleans, has rejected it. The court agreed to hear appeals in all three cases: Epic Systems Corp. v. Lewis, No. 16-258; Ernst & Young v. Morris, No. 16-300; and National Labor Relations Board v. Murphy Oil USA, No. 16-307.

Justice Gorsuch wrote that Congress would not have overridden the arbitration law by using general language in the labor law. "The employees' theory," he wrote, quoting an earlier decision, "runs afoul of the usual rule that Congress 'does not alter the fundamental details of a regulatory scheme in vague terms or ancillary provisions — it does not, one might say, hide elephants in mouseholes.' "

CHAPTER 4

Speaking Up and Speaking Out

Although Ginsburg can be very reserved, she's extremely passionate about her views, and over time she's become more unfiltered about voicing her opinions, even on the other side of the courtroom doors. However, she's encountered public criticism for crossing the line, especially when her personal opinions could conflict with a potential Supreme Court case. She has acknowledged some of these missteps, but despite it all, she's accumulated quite a fan base for her unwavering and often blunt perspective.

In Her Own Words: Ruth Bader Ginsburg

BY THE NEW YORK TIMES | JUNE 15, 1993

ON WOMEN AND THE LAW

From a 1987 speech in Colorado Springs:

THE WARREN COURT of the 1960's thus held the base line set by the Supreme Court in the 1870's, at the turn of the century, and in the 1940's. That base line tied tightly into the prevailing "separate spheres" mentality, or breadwinner-homemaker dichotomy: It was man's lot, because of his nature, to be breadwinner, head of the household, representative of the family outside the home; and it was woman's lot, because of her nature, not only to bear but also to raise children, and keep the home in order.

Against this background, the Supreme Court's position on gender-based classification in the 1970's stands out in bold relief. At odds with its "conservative" reputation, the Burger Court's performance was comparatively unrestrained, one might even say modestly revolutionary, in this area. …

I do not want to leave you with the impression that the judiciary has proceeded automatonlike — securely on course without missteps, detours, inconsistencies and the like. Occasional fog is inevitable in this domain. Registration for the military draft and the statutory rape, to take two 1980's examples, proved perplexing for the Justices. And no bold line waiting to be revealed divides justifiable and genuinely helpful "affirmative action" from action that reinforces the harmful notion that women need a boost or preference, because they cannot make it on their own. A court too sure of itself on these matters may, in its zeal, take a giant stride, only to find itself perilously positioned on an unstable doctrinal limb.

ON RELIGION AND THE MILITARY

From Judge Ginsburg's dissenting opinion in Goldman v. Secretary of Defense, a 1984 decision by the United States Court of Appeals for the District of Columbia that let stand a regulation that banned wearing yarmulkes while on duty:

The plaintiff in this case, S. Simcha Goldman, has long served his country as an Air Force officer with honor and devotion. A military commander has now declared intolerable the yarmulke Dr. Goldman has worn without incident throughout his several years of military service. At the least, the declaration suggests "callous indifference" to Dr. Goldman's religious faith, and it runs counter to "the best of our traditions" to "accommodate the public service to the spiritual needs [of our people]."

ON ROE V. WADE

From a lecture at the New York University School of Law on March 9, 1993:

The effective judge will strive to persuade and not to pontificate. She will speak in "a moderate and restrained voice," engaging in a dialogue with, not a diatribe against, co-equal departments of government, state authorities, and even her own colleagues. …

In writing for the court, one must be sensitive to the sensibilities and mindsets of one's colleagues, which may mean avoiding certain arguments and authorities, even certain words. Should institutional concerns affect the tone of separate opinions, when a judge finds it necessary to write one? …

Measured motions seem to me right, in the main, for constitutional as well as common law adjudication. Doctrinal limbs too swiftly shaped, experience teaches, may prove unstable.

The most prominent example in recent decades is Roe v. Wade. … The 7-2 judgment in Roe v. Wade declared "violative of the due process clause of the 14th Amendment" a Texas criminal abortion statute that "except[ed] from criminality only a life-saving procedure on behalf of the [pregnant woman]." Suppose the Court had stopped there, thus declaring unconstitutional the most extreme brand of law in the nation, and had not gone on, as the Court did in Roe, to fashion a regime blanketing the subject, a set of rules that displaced virtually every state law then in force?

Would there have been the 20-year controversy we have witnessed, reflected most recently in the Supreme Court's splintered decision in Planned Parenthood v. Casey? A less encompassing Roe, I believe and will summarize why, might have served to reduce rather than to fuel controversy.

On Privacy and Equality

BY LINDA GREENHOUSE | JUNE 16, 1993

Judge Ginsburg still voices strong doubts on rationale behind Roe v. Wade ruling.

WASHINGTON, JUNE 15 — Standing by President Clinton's side on Monday afternoon as the first Supreme Court nominee of a Democratic President in a generation, Judge Ruth Bader Ginsburg relied on an unlikely source to explain her judicial philosophy to a public that knew her scarcely, if at all.

She approvingly quoted Chief Justice William H. Rehnquist, a bete noire to Democrats for most of that time, as saying that a good judge is bound to apply the facts and the law to come up with a decision, even if it is "not what the home crowd wants."

It was a telling choice of a quotation that underscored Judge Ginsburg's own seemingly anomalous role as both an authentic heroine in the legal battle for women's rights and a prominent critic of what many see as the crowning accomplishment of that battle, the Supreme Court's decision in Roe v. Wade that established a constitutional right to abortion.

Her criticism of the 1973 decision, expressed over the years but most notably in a lecture at New York University Law School three months ago, has somewhat discomfited her home crowd of feminist lawyers and other leaders of the women's movement. Sound bites suggesting that her commitment to abortion rights is something less than unwavering have been the inevitable result.

DIVIDED ON APPROACH

The difference is not over the ultimate goal of a right to abortion fully anchored in the Constitution and secure against political undermining. Rather, Judge Ginsburg's lecture reflects a long-running debate about whether that goal could have been better achieved by another route, as a matter both of constitutional doctrine and judicial strategy, and over what lessons to draw from the tortuous history of abortion rights in the 20 years since Roe v. Wade was decided.

Judge Ginsburg's critique of Roe v. Wade is twofold. First, she said in the New York University lecture, as she has written for years, the right to abortion might have been more secure had it been grounded in the concept of women's right to equality rather than in the right to privacy. "The Roe decision might have been less of a storm center," she said, had it "homed in more precisely on the women's-equality dimension of the issue."

Given the fact that the right to privacy has become little more than a code word for abortion in current political discourse, it might appear startling to divorce abortion from privacy and seek a home for abortion rights elsewhere in the Constitution.

THE NOTION OF EQUALITY

But the equality argument for abortion rights — essentially the notion that women cannot participate in society equally with men without the ability to control their reproductive lives — was in fact part of the abortion-rights movement from its earliest years. An equality argument was among the arguments presented to the Court in Roe v. Wade.

While Justice Harry A. Blackmun's majority opinion took a different path, a theoretical debate continued in academic legal circles throughout the next decade. Judge Ginsburg, who as a litigator arguing cases before the Supreme Court had helped create the modern constitutional law of women's equality, continued to press for equality.

The argument at times became bitter because of a new element: the proposed equal rights amendment to the Constitution. Some leaders of the long and ultimately unsuccessful campaign for the amendment were concerned that too close a link between equality and abortion would pose a political threat to the E.R.A. by driving away potential supporters of the amendment who did not share the abortion-rights agenda.

In any event, long after the equal rights amendment died and the argument faded into history, it was the Supreme Court itself that revived the equality basis for abortion rights in its ruling last year in Planned Parenthood v. Casey, the Pennsylvania case in which the Court reaffirmed the right to abortion.

STICKING TO THE 'CORE'

Among the reasons that Justices Sandra Day O'Connor, Anthony M. Kennedy and David H. Souter gave in their opinion for adhering to the "core" of Roe v. Wade was a sentence that could have been written by Judge Ginsburg: "The ability of women to participate equally in the economic and social life of the nation has been facilitated by their ability to control their reproductive lives."

The second part of Judge Ginsburg's critique concerns the scope of Roe v. Wade, and it is this part that has made some abortion-rights leaders, including Kate Michelman of the National Abortion Rights Action League, somewhat wary. Judge Ginsburg has argued that by issuing a broad ruling that swept most state abortion laws off the books, the Court created an inherently vulnerable precedent that led to a backlash and short-circuited a liberal trend then under way in the states.

While her New York University lecture discussed Roe v. Wade specifically, her critique reflected a more general approach to judging and to the development of the law. "Measured motions seem to me right, in the main, for constitutional as well as common-law adjudication," she said. "Doctrinal limbs too swiftly shaped, experience teaches, may prove unstable." She praised the Court's opinion last year in Planned Parenthood v. Casey for opening a "renewed dialogue" between the states and the Court.

Marcy Wilder, senior staff lawyer for the abortion-rights league, said in an interview today, "When she says that Roe went too far and that Casey is progress, we have to know whether she's saying that a lesser standard of protection for abortion is a better standard." Ms.

Wilder said it was far from clear historically that most states would have liberalized their abortion laws significantly on their own.

'VISION OF THE FUTURE'?

Helen Neuborne, executive director of the NOW Legal Defense and Educational Fund, also took issue with the notion that a more gradual approach by the Court might have avoided political fallout from the anti-abortion side. There are many possible explanations for the events of the last 20 years, Ms. Neuborne said, including a failure by abortion-rights groups to protect their court victories by early grass-roots organizing.

"These are very complicated issues," Ms. Neuborne said. "She believes that incremental in the long run wins the race. Some of us want everything all the time, all the way. It's a legitimate discussion. Her vision may be the vision of the future. Her gift may be to be able to build and hold the middle of the Court, to accomplish our goals in her style."

This somewhat abstract debate over style and approach will become concrete soon enough if Judge Ginsburg is confirmed. On abortion, for example, the Court has a substantial amount of unfinished business before it in defining the standard the Casey opinion adopted for judging state restrictions on abortion.

The Court said last year that state regulations must not place an "undue burden" on women's access to abortion. By the Court's next term or soon after that, the Justices will be confronted with abortion regulations that have had full trials under the new standard and that pose the question of what burdens are actually "undue."

Judge Ginsburg's written work leaves unclear how she will approach this second-generation abortion debate, and which abortion restrictions she would be most likely to strike down. Justice Byron R. White, to whose seat Judge Ginsburg has been named, never voted to strike down any.

The Unsinkable R.B.G.

OPINION | BY GAIL COLLINS | FEB. 20, 2015

RUTH BADER GINSBURG isn't planning on going anywhere any time soon.

"Now I happen to be the oldest," the 81-year-old justice said in the tone of a person who has answered a whole lot of questions about her possible retirement plans. Sitting in her Supreme Court chambers on a dreary afternoon in late January, she added, "But John Paul Stevens didn't step down until he was 90."

Until recently, when Ginsburg was asked about retiring, she would note that Justice Louis Brandeis had served until he was 82.

"That's getting a little uncomfortable," she admitted.

Over the past few years, she's been getting unprecedented public nagging about retirement while simultaneously developing a massive popular fan base. You can buy T-shirts and coffee mugs with her picture on them. You can dress your baby up like Ruth Bader Ginsburg for Halloween. A blog called Notorious R.B.G. posts everything cool about the justice's life, from celebrity meet-ups ("Sheryl Crow is a Ruth Bader Ginsburg fangirl") to Twitter-size legal theory ("Justice Ginsburg Explains Everything You Need to Know About Religious Liberty in Two Sentences"). You can even get an R.B.G. portrait tattooed on your arm, should the inclination ever arise.

Supreme Court justices used to be known only through their opinions, but in the 21st century they can be celebrities, too. In court, Ginsburg makes headlines with her ferocious dissents against conservative decisions. Outside, the public is reading about her admission that she dozed off at a State of the Union address because she was a little tipsy from wine at dinner. (Plus, she told MSNBC's Irin Carmon, she had been up all the night before, writing: "My pen was hot.") This summer, Ginsburg will attend the premiere of "Scalia/Ginsburg," a one-act opera that the composer Derrick Wang describes as a comedy in which two justices "must pass through three cosmic trials to secure their freedom." Pieces of it have already been performed, and both Ginsburg and the über-conservative justice Antonin Scalia, a fellow opera lover, are apparently really, really pleased.

Hard to imagine any of that happening to John Roberts.

The retirement talk started around 2011, when the Harvard Law School professor Randall Kennedy wrote an essay in The New Republic arguing that both Ginsburg and Justice Stephen Breyer should quit while there was still a Democratic president to nominate replacements. "What's more, both are, well, old," he added uncharitably.

As time moved on, the focus shifted almost exclusively to Ginsburg ("Justice Ginsburg: Resign Already!"). Perhaps that's simply because she is older than Breyer, who is now 76. Or perhaps there's still an expectation that women are supposed to be good sports, and volunteer to take one for the team.

From the beginning, Ginsburg waved off the whole idea. ("And who do you think Obama could have nominated and got confirmed that you'd rather see on a court?") Anyway, since Republicans took control of the Senate in January, it's become pretty clear that ship has sailed.

"People aren't saying it as much now," she said with what sounded like some satisfaction.

Obviously, a time will come. But as far as clarity on the bench, productivity and overall energy go, that time doesn't at all seem to be at hand. Her medical history is studded with near disasters — colon cancer in 1999, and pancreatic cancer 10 years later. Both times she returned to the bench quickly. (In the latter case, Senator Jim Bunning of Kentucky apologized for predicting she'd probably be dead within nine months.) Last year she had a stent placed in one of her coronary arteries. That happened on a Wednesday, and the court's public information officer quickly told reporters that Ginsburg "expects to be on the bench on Monday."

Her physical fierceness is legend. Scalia, her improbable good friend, once recounted a summer when he and Ginsburg had both snagged a gig teaching on the French Riviera. "She went off parasailing!" he told The Washington Post. "This little skinny thing, you'd think she'd never come down." She has since given up that sort of recreation, but she still works out twice a week in the Supreme Court gym with her personal trainer. Plus there are the daily stretching exercises at home. At night. After work.

It's the combination of Ginsburg's woman-hear-me-roar history, her frail-little-old-lady appearance and her role as the leader of the Supreme Court's dissident liberals that have rallied her new fan base, particularly young women.

The second woman to be appointed to the Supreme Court, she's part of the generation who came of age after World War II and led a revolution that transformed women's legal rights, as well as their role in the public world. There's a famous story about the dean at Harvard Law inviting Ginsburg and her tiny group of fellow female law students to dinner, then asking them how they'd justify having taken a place that could have gone to a man. Ginsburg was so flustered she answered that her husband, Marty, was a law student and that it was very important for a wife to understand her husband's work.

"That's what I said," she nodded.

The dean, Ginsburg said, told her later that he had asked only because "there were still doubting Thomases on the faculty and he wanted the women to arm him with stories." You have to wonder if the dean was trying to rewrite history. Or maybe joking. But Ginsburg believed the explanation: "He was a wonderful man, but he had no sense of humor."

During law school Marty Ginsburg developed testicular cancer. Ruth helped him keep up with his work by bringing him notes from his classes and typing up his papers, while also taking care of their toddler, Jane. Plus, she made the Harvard Law Review. This is the kind of story that defines a certain type of New Woman of Ginsburg's generation — people whose gift for overachievement and overcoming adversity is so immense, you can see how even a nation of men bent on maintaining the old patriarchal order were simply run over by the force of their determination. (Ginsburg herself isn't given to romanticizing. Asked why the women's rights revolution happened so quickly, she simply said: "Well, the tide was in our favor. We were riding with winners.")

Ginsburg was married for 56 years — Marty died in 2010. She has a son, a daughter and four grandchildren, one of whom called and said "Bubbe, you were sleeping at the State of the Union!" after the cameras caught her famous nap. She travels constantly. The day we talked, she was preparing to go off to a meeting of the New York City Bar, where she would introduce Gloria Steinem, who would deliver the Justice Ruth Bader Ginsburg Distinguished Lecture on Women and the Law. A few weeks earlier, at a gathering of the Association of American Law Schools, Ginsburg had introduced her old friend Professor Herma Hill Kay, recipient of the Ruth Bader Ginsburg Lifetime Achievement Award. When you reach this kind of stature, there are lots of echoes.

She's spent much of her life being the first woman doing one thing or another, and when it comes to the retirement question, she has only one predecessor to contemplate — her friend Sandra Day O'Connor, the first female Supreme Court justice, who left the bench at 75 to spend more time with her husband, John, who was suffering from Alzheimer's disease.

"She and John were going to do all the outdoorsy things they liked to do," Ginsburg recalled. But John O'Connor's condition deteriorated so swiftly that her plans never worked out. Soon, Ginsburg said, "John was in such bad shape that she couldn't keep him at home."

O'Connor has kept busy — speaking, writing, hearing cases on a court of appeals and pursuing a project to expand civics education. But it's not the same as being the swing vote on the United States Supreme Court. "I think she knows that when she left that term, every 5-4 decision when I was in the minority, I would have been in the majority if she'd stayed," Ginsburg said.

Besides not retiring, another thing Ginsburg is planning not to do is write her memoirs. "There are too many people writing about me already," she said. There's an authorized biography in the works, along with several other projects to which she has definitely not given a blessing.

"But now — this is something I like," she said, picking up a collection of essays, "The Legacy of Ruth Bader Ginsburg." The justice also seems to be looking forward to an upcoming "Notorious R.B.G." book, written by Shana Knizhnik, who created the blog, and Irin Carmon of MSNBC. The name started as a play on the name of the Brooklyn gangsta rapper Notorious B.I.G., but it's taken on a life of its own as a younger-generation tribute to Ginsburg.

"The kind of raw excitement that surrounds her is palpable," Carmon said. "There's a counterintuitiveness. We have a particular vision of someone who's a badass — a 350-pound rapper. And she's this tiny Jewish grandmother. She doesn't look like our vision of power, but she's so formidable, so unapologetic, and a survivor in every sense of the word."

So Ginsburg is planning to be on the bench when the Supreme Court decides mammoth issues like the future of the Affordable Care Act and a national right for gay couples to marry. She says she doesn't know how the health care case will turn out. But like practically every court observer in the country, she has a strong hunch about which way gay marriage will go: "I would be very surprised if the Supreme Court retreats from what it has said about same-sex unions."

The speed with which the country has already accepted gay rights was, she theorized, just a matter of gay people coming out, and the rest of the country realizing that "we all knew and liked and loved people who were gay." She recalled Justice Lewis Powell, who told his colleagues he had never met a gay person, unaware that he'd had several gay law clerks. "But they never broadcast it."

The National Organization for Marriage, a conservative group, recently demanded that Ginsburg recuse herself from the case since she had said that it would not be difficult for the American public to accept a ruling in favor of a national right to gay marriage.

Don't hold your breath.

GAIL COLLINS is an Op-Ed columnist for The New York Times.

Justice Ginsburg's Cautious Radicalism

OPINION | BY IRIN CARMON | OCT. 24, 2015

ONE DAY LAST MAY, while receiving an award, Justice Ruth Bader Ginsburg of the Supreme Court was asked to give advice to her younger female admirers.

It's a question that she has been asked many times, more often these days, as legions of young women have chosen the octogenarian as their quiet-voiced but steel-spined icon. That day onstage, I listened as she seemed to think for a particularly long time before answering.

"My advice is fight for the things that you care about," Justice Ginsburg said. Fair enough — banal enough, really. Then she added, "But do it in a way that will lead others to join you."

It was Ruth Bader Ginsburg's vision, distilled: Have a radical aim, but proceed with caution.

Unlike the Notorious R.B.G. meme, which celebrates the justice by juxtaposing her with the legendary rapper Notorious B.I.G., this message is unlikely to go viral. But our current paralyzed political moment is in dire need of it anyway.

Over the course of Justice Ginsburg's career, she often had no choice but to be the first, but she never wanted to be the only. That meant, as a co-founder of the A.C.L.U. Women's Rights Project, bringing cases that would persuade an all-male Supreme Court that women were equal under the law. It required being a principled but canny fighter. Those qualities are also how we got a feminist hero on the Supreme Court.

This is the irony of Justice Ginsburg's having become a pop culture icon, inspired by her fiery dissents to the conservative majority opinions. Young women have tattooed themselves and painted their nails with the justice's face. They've created tributes in needlepoint, clay, T-shirt and Lego.

Justice Ruth Bader Ginsburg.

Justice Ginsburg has been depicted as an avenging angel smiting her enemies, with two middle fingers up in the air, and as a warrior Athena inked on the arm of more than one feminist. (The justice, generally amused by all this, has told me that she thinks the tattoos go too far.) Spend enough time looking at this fan art and you can get the impression that she is a sort of judicial Carrie Nation, hacking at injustice with a hatchet.

But Justice Ginsburg would prefer a more delicate tool, having no patience for confrontation just for the sake of it. "Anger, resentment, envy and self-pity are wasteful reactions," she has written. "They greatly drain one's time. They sap energy better devoted to productive endeavors."

Only Justice Ginsburg would have added the fairly unpoetic coda to the Rev. Dr. Martin Luther King Jr.'s famous declaration that "the arc of the moral universe is long, but it bends toward justice." It does, she agreed in her oral dissent to an opinion striking down part of the Voting Rights Act in 2013, but said, only "if there is a steadfast commitment to see the task through to completion." No wonder she's refused to retire — she still has work to do.

The arc of Justice Ginsburg's moral universe is still bending. Forty years ago, she imagined a world where men and women were free to pursue their own destinies regardless of gender norms, where men were encouraged to do their part as caregivers and the state didn't interfere with women's reproductive decisions. These are, and remain, profoundly controversial ideas in our society.

But the younger Justice Ginsburg's intentionally unthreatening exterior — married, traditionally feminine, always an impeccable student and scholar — helped mask the intensity and breadth of her convictions. "I think had she not had this persona as this very soft-spoken, neat, and tidy person, with a conventional life, she would have been considered a flaming radical," her friend Cynthia Fuchs Epstein said. She used those relative privileges to work on behalf of others.

The first time Justice Ginsburg argued a case before the Supreme Court, in 1973, she was handed a bar admissions card that read, "Mrs. Ruth Ginsburg." She had gone by Ms. ever since there was a Ms. designation to be used. Her law students, who had helped radicalize their teacher with their refusal to accept gender discrimination, promptly protested. But Professor Ginsburg shrugged it off. She was there to win the case of an Air Force lieutenant whose husband had been denied equal benefits, not to make a fuss over a name card. What the litigator was asking for in her case was a big enough leap. (She won.)

Her vision for the world is transformative, but instead of broad sweeps, she has urged slow, incremental steps to that change. Rather than capitulation, this is about playing a long game. These principles sustained her through decades of experiencing discrimination, and formed her legal strategy. "She insisted that we attempt to develop the law one step at a time," a fellow A.C.L.U. lawyer, Kathleen Peratis, testified at Justice Ginsburg's confirmation hearings in 1993. " 'Present the court with the next logical step,' she urged us, and then the next and then the next. 'Don't ask them to go too far too fast, or you'll lose what you might have won.' She often said, 'It's not time for that case.' We usually followed her advice, and when we didn't, we invariably lost."

On the court, Justice Ginsburg has tranquilly preached collegiality, a savvy move given that she and her colleagues are stuck together for life. In victory, Justice Ginsburg now tells her clerks, never demonize your opponents. She would rather win cases than go out dissenting in glory, which means, she said in a 2012 talk, "an opinion of the court very often reflects views that are not 100 percent what the opinion author would do, were she writing for herself."

All this as her friend Justice Antonin Scalia's fury on the bench has intensified. "I've been known on occasion to suggest that Justice Scalia tone down his dissenting opinions ... because he'll be more effective if he is not so polemical," Justice Ginsburg once said.

It may seem strange for a feminist to counsel against anger when those of us who are not straight, white men have had to fight just to have room to express it. But the risk of burnout over fast-flaming conflicts is real. Our current conversations value catharsis over strategy. This doesn't mean picking the middle point of two poles and calling it common sense; it just means thinking past instant outrage and doing sustainable work.

A former law professor, Justice Ginsburg likes to say she is still a teacher. When I interviewed her, she said her response to experiencing injustice is to "try to teach through my opinions, through my speeches, how wrong it is to judge people on the basis of what they look like, the color of their skin, whether they're men or women."

All of this explains why legal insiders were startled a few years ago when, in Justice Ginsburg terms, she started getting openly angry. As the court lurched to the right, the justice picked battles by sternly dissenting in cases about contraception, voting rights, sex discrimination and remedies for racial discrimination. With affirmative action, labor and reproductive rights poised to return to the court's agenda, we may hear her protest again.

By that point, you can be sure she will have tried everything else. She'll still be fighting for the things she cares about. But this time, she'll be asking us to join her.

IRIN CARMON is a co-author, with Shana Knizhnik, of "Notorious RBG: The Life and Times of Ruth Bader Ginsburg," and a national reporter at MSNBC.

Ruth Bader Ginsburg and Gloria Steinem on the Unending Fight for Women's Rights

TABLE FOR THREE | BY PHILIP GALANES | NOV. 14, 2015

In Table for Three, two celebrities join Philip Galanes for a meal and conversation.

THE ROOM WENT STILL when the women hugged. All of the staff, bustling in preparation just moments before, paused when Ruth Bader Ginsburg emerged quietly from her private chambers at the Supreme Court last month and embraced her old friend Gloria Steinem.

And just as quickly, life resumed. Justice Ginsburg, 82, led Ms. Steinem, 81, into her wood-paneled chambers, with its stately traditional furniture and blue-chip modern art by Mark Rothko and Josef Albers (on loan from the National Gallery of Art and the Hirshhorn Museum and Sculpture Garden). "What a magical place, Ruth," Ms. Steinem said.

Justice Ginsburg gestured to an immaculately set table in the corner, tucked beside shelves of mementos and personal photographs — including one of the two women together. She offered tea, cookies and chocolates she had brought back from a recent trip to Zurich.

These women have a history. Long before she was crowned "Notorious R.B.G." — a nod to the tough-guy rapper Notorious B.I.G. — for her fierce intellect, Justice Ginsburg was a trailblazing litigator for women's rights. Beginning in the early 1970s, as a professor at Columbia Law School, its first tenured woman, and as a founder of the American Civil Liberties Union's Women's Rights Project, she successfully argued five cases before the Supreme Court, focusing on laws and government policies built on gender stereotypes.

At about the same time, Ms. Steinem founded Ms. magazine with some feminist colleagues, after a decade as a journalist in which she tried, and mostly failed, by her account, to interest editors in serious

Justice Ruth Bader Ginsburg, left, and Gloria Steinem in Justice Ginsburg's chambers in the Supreme Court.

articles on women's rights. Still, she published seminal articles, like one detailing her stint as a Playboy bunny to highlight the sexist treatment of women at Playboy Clubs, and a pioneering work in 1969, "After Black Power, Women's Liberation."

Justice Ginsburg was appointed by President Jimmy Carter to the United States Court of Appeals for the District of Columbia Circuit in 1980. In 1993, President Bill Clinton elevated her to the Supreme Court, making her the court's second female justice, following Sandra Day O'Connor. (Justice Ginsburg is the subject of a tribute biography, "Notorious RBG: The Life and Times of Ruth Bader Ginsburg," by Irin Carmon and Shana Knizhnik.)

Meanwhile, Ms. Steinem was an editor at Ms. for nearly 20 years, becoming the public face of the women's movement. (She continues at the magazine as an adviser.) She has traveled extensively, speaking out for women's and human rights, winning numerous awards for her work in media and advocacy, including the Presidential Medal of Freedom in 2013. Her new book, "My Life on the Road," was published last month.

For nearly 90 minutes, the old friends reminisced about their parallel careers and experiences as women, and the work that has made them part of history.

Philip Galanes: Let's start with a glaring inequity. Only one of you has a rap name.

Ruth Bader Ginsburg: I like the way mine began. A second-year law student at N.Y.U. was outraged by the court's decision in the voting rights case. But instead of just venting her anger, she took up my dissent.

PG: Happily, there are rap-name generators online.

Gloria Steinem: They have those?

PG: Yours, if you want it, is GlowStick.

GS: We may need to work on that.

PG: Rap names aside, your careers unfolded side by side at the forefront of the women's movement. When did you meet?

GS: When Ruth was at the A.C.L.U. What comes to mind are these cases in which young African-American women were being sterilized without their permission.

RBG: There was an irony. We couldn't get abortions. But there was this notorious obstetrician, and if it was a woman's third child, he would automatically sterilize her.

GS: The A.C.L.U. would not have taken up that case if it hadn't been for Ruth.

PG: Were you a Ms. reader?

RBG: I certainly was. From the first issue. I thought it was wonderful.

GS: And I knew from other women that Ruth was our champion and teacher.

PG: When you were young, women couldn't rent apartments or get credit cards without men. Did you buy into that?

RBG: Gloria went to Smith; I went to Cornell. It was the school for parents who wanted to make sure their girl would find a man. Four guys for every woman. If you came out without a husband, you were hopeless.

PG: Was Smith more enlightened in the early '50s?

GS: It was a women's college, but the emphasis was on marriage. Even the Smith president of the era said, "We are educating women because to have educated children, we must have educated mothers." The idea that women would do something other than produce children was not out there.

PG: Time for galling stories: Will you tell us more about that dinner of brand-new Harvard law women, when the dean invited all nine of you, from a class of 500, and asked, "How do you justify taking a spot from a qualified man?"

RBG: I was so embarrassed. The dean had each of the women escorted by a distinguished professor. Mine looked more like God than any man I ever met. He was also a chain smoker, so we were sharing an ashtray on my lap. When I stood to speak, the cigarette butts fell on the living-room floor. But I gave him the answer he expected: "My husband is a second-year law student, and it's important for a woman to understand her husband's work."

PG: Did you really think that?

RBG: Of course not!

GS: That's called "Aunt Tom-ing," I think.

RBG: The only thing that really bothered me is they had given me a generous scholarship. We had to take two years off when [my husband] Marty was in the service. And when I applied for readmission, they said, "Submit your father-in-law's financial statement."

GS: You can't make this up.

RBG: They shouldn't give scholarship funds to a person with family money, but you can be sure they never asked a guy to submit his father-in-law's statement.

GS: Or his mother-in-law's.

PG: Now, Gloria's turn: Early in your career, you're sitting in the back of a cab, between Gay Talese and Saul Bellow, and Gay says: "Every year a pretty girl comes to New York and pretends to be a writer. This year, it's Gloria." Any desire to push him out the door?

GS: I had just interviewed Saul Bellow in Chicago, but it wasn't published yet. My first response was, "Oh, he's going to be regretful that he gave an interview to someone who's not really a writer." It wasn't until we were out of the taxi that I got angry. And it wasn't until years later that I got really angry.

PG: But your first thought was to doubt yourself.

GS: And in a weird way, to be fair to Gay Talese, he thought it was a compliment. He didn't see that I wanted to be a serious writer.

PG: Let's take a step back to your mothers, very different women.

From left, Betty Friedan, Elinor Guggenheimer, Eleanor Holmes Norton and Gloria Steinem at an early meeting of the National Women's Political Caucus.

R.B.G.'s pushes her; Gloria's is seriously depressed. Yet these different women raised such independent daughters.

GS: Perhaps we were living out the unlived lives of our mothers. Mine wanted to be a writer and was a journalist long before I was born. First as a reporter, then an editor at a Toledo newspaper.

RBG: My mother was a powerful influence. She made me toe the line. If I didn't have a perfect report card, she showed her disappointment.

PG: Had she been a "perfect report card" kind of girl?

RBG: She told a story about bringing home a report card with all A's to her father. But it didn't mean anything. She was a girl. My mother graduated from high school at 15 and went to work to support the family because the eldest son went to college.

GS: So you were receiving her dreams. She was saying the opposite to you: not that your report card didn't count, but that it did.

RBG: She wanted me to be independent. And what she meant was becoming a high school history teacher because she never dreamed there would be other opportunities.

PG: Did you?

RBG: Not at the time.

PG: Choosing law and political reporting was uncommon for women in the '50s. Did you have mentors helping you?

GS: In a word, no. For me, writing was a way of staying invisible because I felt invisible, only a little seen through words. I didn't yet have the courage to speak up.

PG: Was your family supportive?

GS: My mother worried about me economically. But my father had inadvertently prepared me well to be a freelance writer by being such a free spirit and never having a regular job.

RBG: My mother was dead by then, and my father was very worried because he couldn't support me. Then I married Marty the month I graduated from college, and it was all fine. I could go off to law school. If nobody hired me, I had a man to support me.

PG: Weirdly, he was right. No one hired the woman who graduated No. 1 in her class.

RBG: There were many firms who put up sign-up sheets that said,

"Men Only." And I had three strikes against me. First, I was Jewish, and the Wall Street firms were just beginning to accept Jews. Then I was a woman. But the killer was my daughter Jane, who was 4 by then.

PG: They didn't even hide why they were rejecting you?

GS: No. I tried to get a much less prestigious job, at Time magazine. And they made it very clear that women researched, and men wrote. No exceptions, in spite of Clare Boothe Luce.

PG: You remind me of my grandmother's line: Rejection is the best thing that can happen. It pushes us. There might not be a Ms. magazine or Notorious R.B.G. without it.

GS: But there might not be a need for a woman's magazine, and there might be a court that actually looks like the country. There's no virtue in injustice.

RBG: Justice O'Connor once said: "Suppose there had been no discrimination when we finished law school. We'd be retired partners from large law firms today." She got her first job working for free for a county attorney, and she was very high in her class at Stanford.

GS: The great thing about obstacles is that they cause you to identify with other groups of people who are facing obstacles.

PG: When did you start thinking seriously about women's equality?

RBG: When I was working on a book about civil procedure in Sweden, in 1962 and '63.

GS: For which she learned Swedish. Is that not incredible?

RBG: Between 20 and 25 percent of the law students in Sweden were women. And there were women on the bench. I went to one proceeding in Stockholm where the presiding judge was eight months pregnant. There was also a journalist who wrote a column in the Swedish daily paper: "Why should women have two jobs, and men only one?" Inflation was high, and two incomes were often needed. But it was the woman who was expected to buy the kids new shoes and have dinner on the table at 7. I remember listening to those conversations. It was that same summer I read "The Second Sex."

GS: For me, an important point came when I was living in India, because of the Gandhian movement and the role of women in it. But I was slow to see how it applied here. I couldn't quite bridge that gap until the late '60s.

PG: How did people respond when you first raised concerns about equality for women?

GS: They were either disinterested or said it was impossible. My classic experience was an editor who said, "O.K., you can publish an article saying women are equal." But right next to it, he would publish an article that said that they weren't — to be objective.

RBG: The concern was that if a woman was doing gender equality, her chances of making it to tenure in the law school were diminished. It was considered frivolous.

GS: I remember covering a hearing in Albany about liberalizing the abortion laws. This was before Roe v. Wade. And they invited to testify 14 men and one nun. A group of women said: "Wait a minute. Let's have our own testimony from women who had this experience." That was my epiphany. But when I wrote about it, my friends at New York magazine, good people, took me aside and said: "You've worked so hard to be taken seriously. Don't get involved with these crazy women."

RBG: The thing that disturbed me was when people would say: "What are those women doing? They're just riding the coattails of the civil rights movement." Yet this change was occurring all over the world, even in homogeneous places, like Sweden, where there were no racial differences. Of course, there was tremendous inspiration from the civil rights movement, and for me, particularly the way Thurgood Marshall led that campaign.

GS: It's important to say that the women's movement was disproportionately pioneered by black women. These are not two different movements; they are profoundly connected. If you are going to continue racism, you have to control reproduction. And that means controlling women. A group called Feminist.com made these baby bead bracelets. On one, they spell "Imagine," and on the other, they asked us to write what we want. I went with "Imagine" and "We are linked, not ranked."

RBG: It's a facet of the gay rights movement that people don't think about enough. Why suddenly marriage equality? Because it wasn't until 1981 that the court struck down Louisiana's "head and master rule," that the husband was head and master of the house. Marriage was a relationship between the dominant, breadwinning husband and the subordinate, child-rearing wife. What lesbian or gay man would want that?

GS: Exactly. Marriage had to change before it could apply to more equal relationships.

PG: What made you enter an institution like that?

RBG: Marty was an extraordinary man. He was so secure in himself that he never regarded me as any kind of threat. He was my biggest booster.

PG: And a brilliant tax lawyer.

RBG: We decided when we met — I was 17, he was 18 — that we were going to be together, whether it was in medicine —

PG: Wait! You decided that you would go into the same profession?

RBG: Right. But Marty had a consuming interest in golf and played on the Cornell golf team. So medicine was out because chemistry labs were in the afternoon. For some reason, he wanted to go to Harvard, and the business school wasn't taking women. So that left law.

GS: It's such an important point for young people, who often think life has to be all planned out. It's not that way.

PG: Did you decide marriage wasn't for you?

GS: Absolutely not. I assumed I had to get married. Everybody did. If you didn't, you were crazy. But I kept putting it off: "I'm going to do it, but not right now." Until I was in my late 30s and the women's movement came along, and I realized: I'm happy. Not everyone has to live the same way.

RBG: I just read Anne-Marie Slaughter's book. She talked about "we don't have it all." Who does? I've had it all in the course of my life, but at different times.

GS: And the implication for women having it all is doing it all. But you can't. We're still far away from the idea of truly shared parenting.

PG: One of the cleverest things you did as a litigator was demonstrate how rigid gender roles harm men as much as women.

RBG: There was an interesting case this court decided in the first year Justice O'Connor was on the bench, about a man who wanted to go to the best nursing school in his area, but it was women-only. You could read between the lines what she understood: There was no better way to raise pay for women in nursing than to get men to do it.

GS: Equal pay for women would be the biggest economic stimulus this country could ever have. Big-time profits are being made from gender roles as they exist. It would also be win-win because female-headed households are where children are most likely to be poor.

PG: Last subject: You are both bridge builders. Justice Ginsburg on the court; and Gloria, with a sea of men and women over the years. Any advice for getting along with people who disagree with us to the core — like Justice Scalia?

RBG: Last night, my daughter and I got a prize from a women's intellectual property group, and Nino [Scalia] was in the video, saying his nice things about me. He's a very funny man. We both love opera. And we care about writing. His style is spicy, but we care about how we say it.

GS: I think Ruth is better at getting along with people with whom we profoundly disagree. I feel invisible in their presence because I'm being treated as invisible. But what we want in the future will only happen if we do it every day. So, kindness matters enormously. And empathy. Finding some point of connection.

RBG: Sometimes not listening helps, too. Do you know about this opera "Scalia/Ginsburg" by a talented musician who went to law school? Scalia's opening aria is: "The Justices are blind. How can they possibly spout this? The Constitution says nothing about this." And I answer: "You are searching in vain for a bright-line solution for a problem that isn't so easy to solve. But the beautiful thing about our Constitution is that, like our society, it can evolve." Then she goes into a jazzy part. Let it grow.

This interview has been edited and condensed.

Ruth Bader Ginsburg, No Fan of Donald Trump, Critiques Latest Term

BY ADAM LIPTAK | JULY 10, 2016

WASHINGTON — Unless they have a book to sell, Supreme Court justices rarely give interviews. Even then, they diligently avoid political topics. Justice Ruth Bader Ginsburg takes a different approach.

These days, she is making no secret of what she thinks of a certain presidential candidate.

"I can't imagine what this place would be — I can't imagine what the country would be — with Donald Trump as our president," she said. "For the country, it could be four years. For the court, it could be — I don't even want to contemplate that."

It reminded her of something her husband, Martin D. Ginsburg, a prominent tax lawyer who died in 2010, would have said.

" 'Now it's time for us to move to New Zealand,' " Justice Ginsburg said, smiling ruefully.

In an interview in her chambers on Friday, Justice Ginsburg took stock of a tumultuous term and chastised the Senate for refusing to act on President Obama's Supreme Court nominee.

Her colleagues have said nothing in public about the presidential campaign or about Mr. Obama's stalled nomination of Judge Merrick B. Garland to the Supreme Court. But Justice Ginsburg was characteristically forthright, offering an unequivocal endorsement of Judge Garland.

"I think he is about as well qualified as any nominee to this court," she said. "Super bright and very nice, very easy to deal with. And super prepared. He would be a great colleague."

Asked if the Senate had an obligation to assess Judge Garland's qualifications, her answer was immediate.

"That's their job," she said. "There's nothing in the Constitution that says the president stops being president in his last year."

The court has been short-handed since Justice Antonin Scalia died in February, and Justice Ginsburg said it will probably remain that way through most or all of its next term, which starts in October. Even in "the best case," in which Judge Garland was confirmed in the lame-duck session of Congress after the presidential election on Nov. 8, she said, he will have missed most of the term's arguments and so could not vote in those cases.

Justice Ginsburg, 83, said she would not leave her job "as long as I can do it full steam." But she assessed what is at stake in the presidential election with the precision of an actuary, saying that Justices Anthony M. Kennedy and Stephen G. Breyer are no longer young.

"Kennedy is about to turn 80," she said. "Breyer is going to turn 78."

For the time being and under the circumstances, she said, the Supreme Court is doing what it can. She praised Chief Justice John G. Roberts Jr.

"He had a hard job," Justice Ginsburg said. "I think he did it quite well."

It was a credit to the eight-member court that it deadlocked only four times, she said, given the ideological divide between its liberal and conservative wings, both with four members.

One of the 4-4 ties, Friedrichs v. California Teachers Association, averted what would have been a severe blow to public unions had Justice Scalia participated. "This court couldn't have done better than it did," Justice Ginsburg said of the deadlock. When the case was argued in January, the majority seemed prepared to overrule a 1977 precedent that allowed public unions to charge nonmembers fees to pay for collective bargaining.

A second deadlock, in United States v. Texas, left in place a nationwide injunction blocking Mr. Obama's plan to spare more than four million unauthorized immigrants from deportation and allow them to work. That was unfortunate, Justice Ginsburg said, but it could have been worse.

"Think what would have happened had Justice Scalia remained with us," she said. Instead of a single sentence announcing the tie, she suggested, a five-justice majority would have issued a precedent-setting decision dealing a lasting setback to Mr. Obama and the immigrants he had tried to protect.

Justice Ginsburg noted that the case was in an early stage and could return to the Supreme Court. "By the time it gets back here, there will be nine justices," she said.

She also assessed whether the court might have considered a narrow ruling rejecting the suit, brought by Texas and 25 other states, on the ground that they had not suffered the sort of direct and concrete injury that gave them standing to sue. Some of the chief justice's writings suggested that he might have found the argument attractive.

"That would have been hard for me," Justice Ginsburg said, "because I've been less rigid than some of my colleagues on questions of standing. There was a good argument to be made, but I would not have bought that argument because of the damage it could do" in other cases.

The big cases the court did decide, on abortion and affirmative action, were triumphs, Justice Ginsburg said. Both turned on Justice Kennedy's vote. "I think he comes out as the great hero of this term," Justice Ginsburg said.

The affirmative action case, Fisher v. University of Texas, was decided by just seven justices, 4 to 3. Justice Elena Kagan had recused herself because she had worked on the case as United States solicitor general.

But Justice Ginsburg said the decision was built to last. "If Justice Kagan had been there, it would have been 5 to 3," she said. "That's about as solid as you can get."

"I don't expect that we're going to see another affirmative action case," Justice Ginsburg added, "at least in education."

The abortion decision, Whole Woman's Health v. Hellerstedt, in a 5-to-3 vote, struck down two parts of a restrictive Texas law, ones requiring doctors who perform abortions to have admitting privileges at nearby hospitals and abortion clinics to meet the demanding standards of ambulatory surgical centers.

Justice Kennedy had only once before voted to find an abortion restriction unconstitutional, in Planned Parenthood v. Casey in 1992, when he joined Justices Sandra Day O'Connor and David H. Souter to save the core of Roe v. Wade, the 1973 decision that established a constitutional right to abortion.

Asked if she had been pleased and surprised by Justice Kennedy's vote in the Texas case, Justice Ginsburg responded: "Of course I was pleased, but not entirely surprised. I know abortion cases are very hard for him, but he was part of the troika in Casey."

Justice Breyer wrote the methodical majority opinion in the Texas case, and Justice Ginsburg added only a brief, sharp concurrence.

"I wanted to highlight the point that it was perverse to portray this as protecting women's health," she said of the challenged requirements. "Desperate women then would be driven to unsafe abortions."

The decision itself, she said, had a message that transcended the particular restrictions before the court.

"It says: 'No laws that are meant to deny a woman her right to choose,' " she said.

Asked if there were cases she would like to see the court overturn before she leaves it, she named one.

"It won't happen," she said. "It would be an impossible dream. But I'd love to see Citizens United overruled."

She mulled whether the court could revisit its 2013 decision in Shelby County v. Holder, which effectively struck down a key part of the Voting Rights Act. She said she did not see how that could be done.

The court's 2008 decision in District of Columbia v. Heller, establishing an individual right to own guns, may be another matter, she said.

"I thought Heller was "a very bad decision," she said, adding that a chance to reconsider it could arise whenever the court considers a challenge to a gun control law.

Should Judge Garland or another Democratic appointee join the court, Justice Ginsburg will find herself in a new position, and the thought seemed to please her.

"It means that I'll be among five more often than among four," she said.

Ruth Bader Ginsburg Regrets Speaking Out on Colin Kaepernick

BY ADAM LIPTAK | OCT. 14, 2016

WASHINGTON — Justice Ruth Bader Ginsburg issued a statement on Friday expressing regret for her critical comments on protests by San Francisco 49ers quarterback Colin Kaepernick and other National Football League players seeking to draw attention to police brutality and racial injustice.

In an interview published Monday, she had called the players' decision to kneel during the national anthem dumb and disrespectful. On Friday, she said she should have held her tongue.

"Some of you have inquired about a book interview in which I was asked how I felt about Colin Kaepernick and other N.F.L. players who refused to stand for the national anthem," she wrote in a note to reporters. "Barely aware of the incident or its purpose, my comments were inappropriately dismissive and harsh. I should have declined to respond."

It was the second time this year that Justice Ginsburg has disavowed public comments. In July, after a series of interviews expressing disdain for Donald J. Trump, she issued a similar statement.

The recent comments came in an interview with Katie Couric of Yahoo News. Justice Ginsburg was there to discuss a new book, and Ms. Couric asked about the protests. "Would I arrest them for doing it?" Justice Ginsburg said of players. "No."

But she added: "I think it's dumb and disrespectful. I would have the same answer if you asked me about flag burning. I think it's a terrible thing to do, but I wouldn't lock a person up for doing it. I would point out how ridiculous it seems to me to do such an act."

Mr. Kaepernick's protests have also drawn criticism from Mr. Trump, who said, "I think it's a terrible thing, and you know, maybe he should find a country that works better for him."

On the other hand, President Obama has said that Mr. Kaepernick has been drawing attention to "some real, legitimate issues" and "exercising his constitutional right."

Speaking to reporters Tuesday in the 49ers locker room, Mr. Kaepernick said Justice Ginsburg had shown a lack of sensitivity. "It is disappointing to hear a Supreme Court justice call a protest against injustices and oppression 'stupid, dumb' in reference to players doing that," he said.

He said he was reading an article that he said referred to "the white critique of black protests and how they try to delegitimize it by calling it 'idiotic, dumb, stupid,' things of that nature, so they can side-step the real issue. As I was reading that, I saw more and more truth how this has been approached by people in power and white people in power in particular."

Justice Ginsburg's statement suggested that she had taken the wrong tone because she had not been fully informed. In expressing regret about her earlier statements, about Mr. Trump, she said only that she should not have uttered them.

"On reflection, my recent remarks in response to press inquiries were ill-advised and I regret making them," she said in July of the Trump remarks. "Judges should avoid commenting on a candidate for public office."

"In the future," Justice Ginsburg said then, "I will be more circumspect."

Justice Ginsburg Urges New Citizens to Make America Better

BY LIZ ROBBINS | APRIL 10, 2018

BEDECKED IN A multicolored collar that reflected the diversity of the 201 new citizens before her, Supreme Court Justice Ruth Bader Ginsburg presided over a naturalization ceremony on Tuesday at the New-York Historical Society, treating her rapt audience to a history lesson, one crackling with life and liberty.

Justice Ginsburg told them that her own father arrived in this country at 13 with no fortune and no ability to speak English, and yet, she would soon be administering the oath of citizenship to them as a member of the highest court in the land.

Across the packed rows of seats at the historical society's Upper West Side theater sat people from 59 countries, with first names like Islam, Hussein, Kazi, Angie and Sunday, and with professions as diverse as pastors and pediatric cancer doctors. Two men from Guinea sat in the third row and learned they were both named Mamadou Alpha Diallo, both taxi drivers.

"We are a nation made strong by people like you," Justice Ginsburg said.

It seemed only appropriate that the Brooklyn-born jurist known by her fans as the Notorious R.B.G. (a play on the rapper Notorious B.I.G.) delivered her remarks at the oldest museum in the city. Justice Ginsburg, 85, is believed to be the first Supreme Court justice to take part in a naturalization ceremony in New York in recent years, even though the court does not keep detailed records of officiating appearances.

"Because I've seen her on the news and the wonderful things she has done for people and now getting to see her live, I had tears coming down my eyes," said Sunday Aito, 50, originally from Nigeria.

Despite the contentious climate surrounding immigration — and who gets admission to the country — Justice Ginsburg made no mention

Ruth Bader Ginsburg, associate justice of the Supreme Court, center, was believed to be the first member of the court to preside over a naturalization ceremony in New York in recent years.

of the Trump administration in her remarks. The Supreme Court will hear arguments this year about the legality of President Trump's travel ban; in a December Supreme Court decision that allowed the third version to continue during the legal challenges, both Justices Ginsburg and Sonia Sotomayor dissented.

Justice Ginsburg will mark her 25th year on the bench in August.

After officiating at the ceremony, she went upstairs in the museum for a private talk with young fellows from the Immigrant Justice Corps, a program for immigration lawyers and practitioners founded in New York by Robert A. Katzmann, the chief judge of the United States Court of Appeals for the Second Circuit.

To preside over a naturalization ceremony at the historical society was Justice Ginsburg's idea.

She said in a statement that she had read a New York Times article about a program at the historical society for citizenship applicants. "I thought it was a grand idea," Justice Ginsburg said. "So, I wrote to N.Y.H.S. and said if ever I am in town when they had a naturalization ceremony, I would be glad to participate."

The Citizenship Project offers free classes to green card holders who are studying for the naturalization test, involving art, documents and artifacts at the museum. Since it began in July 2017, more than 600 people have completed the classes, said its president, Louise Mirrer, and the museum hopes to reach 1,000 by July.

Ms. Mirrer was struck by the compact, powerful civics lesson Justice Ginsburg delivered. "She was careful to present this nation as one that is heavily into self-improvement," Ms. Mirrer said.

In her remarks Justice Ginsburg detailed the evolving history of representation and inclusion, from the preamble to the Constitution to the abolition of slavery to the amendments that allowed women and blacks to vote.

"Alexis de Tocqueville wrote that the greatness of America lies not in being more enlightened than other nations, but rather in her ability to repair her faults," Justice Ginsburg said.

Justice Ginsburg acknowledged that the United States was at its outset an imperfect union, and is still beset by poverty, low voting numbers and by the "struggle to achieve greater understanding of each other across racial, religious and socio-economic lines."

She urged its newest citizens to vote and to foster unity. "We have made huge progress, but the work of perfection is scarcely done," she said.

As a champion of women's rights and equality, Justice Ginsburg proved inspirational to men and women in the audience. Pranitha Mantrala, 35, a physician originally from India, said the message was clear: "I think we can achieve anything."

She became a citizen along with her husband, Srikanth Ambati, 38, who is a pediatric cancer specialist at Memorial-Sloan Kettering Cancer Center. "It meant a lot for me, especially her parents coming from such a background, and her going into such a high profession," Dr. Mantrala said. "It's adorable."

Yusif Abubakari, 42, born in Ghana, was struck by Justice Ginsburg's "humbleness," he said. "She is supposed to be at home but she came because of me, because of us, and that made me feel so special today," Mr. Abubakari said, adding, "May God bless her and give her more life and prosperity."

CHAPTER 5

In Sickness and in Health

Failing health has been a prominent concern in Ginsburg's life. She's fallen and broken three of her ribs. She's had a heart procedure and numerous cancer scares. Although this has prompted concerns about her longevity as a justice, Ginsburg's body and mind have held strong despite the immense pressure from the public and her own body. She's continued to heal and return to the courtroom as sharp and resilient as ever, showing that her age and health concerns cannot keep her from the bench for long.

Ruth Ginsburg Has Surgery for Cancer

BY LINDA GREENHOUSE | SEPT. 18, 1999

JUSTICE RUTH BADER GINSBURG of the Supreme Court was operated on for colon cancer here today, the Supreme Court announced.

Justice Ginsburg's surgeon, Dr. Lee Smith, expected her to remain at Washington Hospital Center for about a week, Kathy Arberg, the court's public information officer, said in a statement.

Ms. Arberg said no further information was available about Justice Ginsburg's condition, any follow-up treatment or when she was likely to return to work at the Court.

The Court's new term begins on Oct. 4.

Justice Ginsburg, who is 66, became ill this summer while teaching in a law school program on the Greek island of Crete. She was hospitalized there and told, incorrectly, that she had acute diverticulitis, the Court statement said. Colon cancer and diverticulitis, a disorder of the large intestine in which pouches that form on the outside of the colon become infected, can sometimes be indistinguishable without extensive tests.

After the diagnosis, Justice Ginsburg returned to work at the Court. Her condition was diagnosed correctly this week, the statement said.

A White House spokesman, David C. Leavy, said tonight: "The President is confident that Judge Ginsburg will confront this latest challenge with the same courage, determination and success that she has shown throughout her extraordinary life. The President and First Lady, on behalf of the American people, hope for a speedy and complete recovery."

Justice Ginsburg was named by President Clinton in 1993 to become the second woman to serve on the nation's highest court. She previously was a judge on the United States Court of Appeals for the District of Columbia Circuit.

Before that, she was a law professor at Rutgers and Columbia law schools, and a leading courtroom advocate for women's rights.

In the past, when justices have missed arguments because of illness, they have occasionally participated in cases after listening to recordings of the arguments. More often, the remaining eight justices have decided the cases, and those in which there has been a 4-4 split have been reargued when the absent justice returned.

Other current justices have had cancer. Justice Sandra Day O'Connor had surgery for breast cancer in 1988, and Justice John Paul Stevens underwent radiation treatment for prostate cancer in 1992.

Whether Justice Ginsburg will need chemotherapy or radiation in addition to the operation she underwent will depend largely on what doctors call a staging system. The system is intended to provide a guide to the extent of spread, if any, of the cancer in the affected area. Doctors rely heavily on such staging systems to give prognoses.

The specific information needed for staging comes from a pathologist's examination through a microscope of the colon cancer and the nearby lymph nodes that were removed at surgery.

Pathologists routinely look at how deeply the cancer has penetrated the walls of the tubular bowel, or through it into adjacent tissues. The doctors also look for the presence of cancerous cells in the lymph nodes.

Additional tests may be performed on the cancerous tissue to determine special characteristics of its basic molecular makeup.

Justice Ginsburg is among the estimated 67,000 women whose colon and rectal cancer will be diagnosed in the United States this year, accounting for 11 percent of all cancers in women, the American Cancer Society says.

Colon and rectal cancer is the third-leading cancer among women. It ranks behind breast and lung cancer in terms of newly diagnosed cases and behind lung and breast cancer in terms of deaths.

Colon and rectal cancer is highly curable when detected early. But recent surveys have found that nearly half of women 50 and older have never been tested for the disease.

The American Cancer Society recommends that women and men 50 and older get one of the following: a test of stool for trace amounts of blood and a sigmoidoscopic examination of the lower bowel every five years; a colonoscopy, or examination of the entire colon, every 10 years, or a barium enema X-ray every 5 to 10 years.

Ginsburg Leaves Hospital; Prognosis on Cancer Is Good

BY SHERYL GAY STOLBERG | SEPT. 29, 1999

THE COLON CANCER diagnosed in Justice Ruth Bader Ginsburg has apparently not spread, and was discovered at an early stage by accident because the Justice suffered symptoms from an unrelated abdominal infection, the Supreme Court announced today.

The 66-year-old Justice went home from Washington Hospital Center today, 11 days after surgeons removed her sigmoid colon, a two-foot length of bowel that makes up the lower third of the large intestine. Doctors have classified her cancer as being in the second of four stages; about 75 percent of Stage 2 colon cancer patients are cured, experts say.

"The Justice is very lucky to have had this picked up incidentally," said Dr. Harmon Eyre, chief medical officer for the American Cancer Society. "If it had been left alone, it would have advanced to another stage."

In a written statement, the Court's public information officer, Kathleen Arberg, said a small tumor, measuring about 2 centimeters by 3 centimeters, had invaded the Justice's colon and entered the outer muscle but did not penetrate through it. Subsequent tests showed no evidence that the disease had spread to the lymph nodes or any other organ.

The tests results are a good sign, Dr. Eyre said, but they are no guarantee. In some patients, he said, "there can be microscopic spread" that does not turn up in early biopsies.

Justice Ginsburg became ill this summer while teaching in a law school program on the Greek island of Crete. Doctors at first thought she had acute diverticulitis, a disorder of the large intestine, but later diagnosed colon cancer.

Now, it turns out, the diverticulitis diagnosis may have been correct after all; according to Ms. Arberg's statement, Dr. Lee Smith, the surgeon at Washington Hospital Center who performed the Sept. 17 operation on Justice Ginsburg, also discovered a perforation higher in her bowel. The perforation, which was not malignant, caused her abdominal infection.

Despite her hospitalization, Justice Ginsburg has been participating in the Court's recent work, although whether she has been involved by telephone, written memo or in some other way was unclear. The Court today issued a list of nine cases that it intended to hear this term; there was no announcement that Justice Ginsburg was absent, as is customary.

Dr. Eyre said most patients in Justice Ginsburg's condition needed at least a month to six weeks to recuperate from surgery, possibly longer in her case if there were complications from the perforated bowel. She should heal completely, he said, without any need for a colostomy, and may not need any chemotherapy or radiation. Doctors should make that determination after evaluating samples of her cancerous tissue.

Ginsburg Has Surgery for Pancreatic Cancer

BY ADAM LIPTAK | FEB. 5, 2009

JUSTICE RUTH BADER GINSBURG underwent surgery at the Memorial Sloan-Kettering Cancer Center in New York on Thursday for what was apparently early-stage pancreatic cancer, according to a statement released by the Supreme Court.

The surgery followed the discovery of a lesion during an annual checkup in late January at the National Institutes of Health in Bethesda, Md. A scan revealed a small tumor, approximately one centimeter across, in the center of the pancreas, the court's statement said.

Dr. Murray F. Brennan, the attending surgeon, said Justice Ginsburg would most likely remain in the hospital for 7 to 10 days, the statement added. A spokeswoman for Sloan-Kettering declined to elaborate.

Justice Ginsburg was treated for colon cancer in 1999 and did not miss a day on the bench. The court next hears arguments on Feb. 23.

According to the American Cancer Society, pancreatic cancer has one of the lowest five-year survival rates, at about 5 percent over all for all stages.

The rate for lung cancer is about 15 percent, and the rates for colon and rectal cancers are 64 percent. The survival rate for pancreatic cancer is so low because the disease is often not diagnosed until its later stages. There is no test for early detection, and such symptoms as weight loss and abdominal discomfort are often overlooked.

Justice Ginsburg, currently the sole woman on the Supreme Court, is the second woman to serve on the court. Justice Sandra Day O'Connor, who was appointed by President Ronald Reagan in 1981, retired in 2005. Justice O'Connor herself underwent surgery for breast cancer in 1988.

Other justices have also battled cancer in recent memory. Justice John Paul Stevens underwent radiation treatment for prostate cancer in 1992. Chief Justice William H. Rehnquist's thyroid cancer was diagnosed 11 months before his death in September 2005.

Justice Ginsburg, 75, was appointed to the court in 1993 by President Bill Clinton. She is a member of the court's liberal wing.

Her appointment ended a 26-year gap during which no Democratic president made an appointment to the Supreme Court. The last justice named by a Democratic president before her was Justice Thurgood Marshall, appointed by President Lyndon B. Johnson in 1967. Mr. Clinton also appointed Justice Stephen G. Breyer, in 1994.

Justice Ginsburg was born in Brooklyn in 1933, graduated from Cornell in 1954 and first attended law school at Harvard, where she was on the law review. After moving to New York with her husband, she transferred to Columbia, joining its law review as well.

She taught at Columbia and Rutgers, and was a leading courtroom advocate for women's rights. As director of the Women's Rights Project of the American Civil Liberties Union in the 1970s, she brought a series of cases before the court that helped establish constitutional protections against sex discrimination.

Her incremental litigation strategy invited comparison to Marshall, the architect of the civil rights movement's legal attack on race discrimination before joining the court.

Before her appointment to the court, Justice Ginsburg served for 13 years as a judge on the United States Court of Appeals for the District of Columbia Circuit.

President Obama was informed of Justice Ginsburg's situation early Thursday afternoon. Robert Gibbs, the White House spokesman, said: "He has not talked with the justice, but his thoughts and prayers are with her and her family right now. We hope for and wish her a speedy recovery."

Even before Mr. Obama took office, he and his top aides had anticipated that they might have a Supreme Court vacancy to fill after the court's current term ends, a senior White House adviser said. Justice Ginsburg's cancer surgery reinforces that view and adds new elements.

If Justice Ginsburg is forced from the court for health reasons, it would increase the possibility of a second vacancy from among her aging colleagues, like Justice John Paul Stevens, who will turn 89 in April.

In preparation for a vacancy, senior Obama advisers have already discussed possible candidates. Many lawyers and court scholars believe that Mr. Obama would be obliged to choose a woman as his first court selection. If Justice Ginsburg were to leave the court, the political imperative to choose a woman would only increase.

Among women on the list of possible candidates are Sonia Sotomayor, a federal appeals court judge in New York; Diane P. Wood, a federal appeals court judge in Chicago; and Elena Kagan, who was the dean at Harvard Law School and was recently nominated to be solicitor general.

Other possible candidates, say court watchers, academics and lawyers, is Deval Patrick, the governor of Massachusetts, a friend of Mr. Obama and a former Justice Department official; Harold Hongju Koh, the dean of the Yale Law School; and Merrick B. Garland, a federal appeals court judge in Washington.

The list also includes Cass R. Sunstein, a law professor at Harvard and former colleague of Mr. Obama at the University of Chicago Law School who has been named administrator of the Office of Information and Regulatory Affairs.

NEIL A. LEWIS and **ANAHAD O'CONNOR** contributed reporting.

Justice Ruth Bader Ginsburg Hospitalized With 3 Broken Ribs

BY EILEEN SULLIVAN | NOV. 8, 2018

WASHINGTON — Justice Ruth Bader Ginsburg, a critical liberal voice on the Supreme Court, was hospitalized on Thursday morning with three broken ribs after falling in her office the day before.

Justice Ginsburg, 85, went home after her fall on Wednesday evening and experienced discomfort during the night, a Supreme Court spokeswoman, Kathy Arberg, said in a statement. She was admitted to George Washington University Hospital on Thursday morning for observation and treatment. Doctors found three broken ribs on her left side.

The next sitting of the Supreme Court begins Nov. 26, and Justice Ginsburg's history suggests the injuries are not likely to keep her away. She broke two ribs in 2012, without missing work. And she returned to work quickly after undergoing a heart procedure in 2012. She is also a cancer survivor and returned to work less than three weeks after having surgery.

Justice Ginsburg is the linchpin of the four-member liberal minority on a Supreme Court that has shifted ideologically to the right under President Trump. In less than two years in office, he has appointed two justices, and he has vowed to fill any further openings with more staunch conservatives. A third Trump appointment to the court would give it a dominant 6-to-3 conservative majority.

Justice Ginsburg is the court's oldest member, a reality not lost on liberals who had already been jittery about how much more time she will be able to serve.

"I think all there is to say at this point is that I — and hopefully all of us — wish Justice Ginsburg all of the best for a full and speedy recovery," said Erwin Chemerinsky, the dean of the law school at the University of California, Berkeley.

Broken ribs are usually painful, and could puncture the lung, depending on the specifics of the break. Ms. Arberg, the court's spokeswoman, did not provide additional details about how Justice Ginsburg fell or whether she fell because of another medical condition. Broken ribs typically take about six weeks to heal, but it varies from case to case.

By midday, Mr. Trump had not publicly commented on Justice Ginsburg's hospitalization. In the morning, the president attended a formal ceremony at the Supreme Court for Justice Brett M. Kavanaugh, who was sworn in last month. All of the other justices were there except for Justice Ginsburg.

Mr. Trump has been critical of Justice Ginsburg, saying in 2016 that "her mind is shot" and suggesting that she resign. His sharp words came after Justice Ginsburg mocked Mr. Trump in a series of interviews. She later said she had made a mistake in publicly commenting on a candidate and promised to be more "circumspect" in the future.

Justice Ginsburg was appointed to the court by President Bill Clinton in 1993. Originally from New York, she speaks with a hint of a Brooklyn accent and once described herself as "this little tiny little woman."

The justice, who is known for her lifetime of work fighting for women's rights, was the subject of a documentary over the summer, and Hollywood is making a movie from her life story. She gained social media popularity in recent years with her own meme and nickname, "Notorious R.B.G." As the news about Justice Ginsburg spread on social media on Thursday, some Twitter users volunteered to donate their ribs to her, and others called for protective bubble wrap to be sent her way.

During the Obama administration, Professor Chemerinsky and other liberals called for Justice Ginsburg to step down sometime during the summer before the 2014 midterm elections so that Mr. Obama could name her successor. The Democrats went on to cede control of the Senate — and thus the ability to confirm Supreme Court justices — in those elections.

When Justice Antonin Scalia died in 2016, Mr. Obama nominated a centrist appellate judge, Merrick B. Garland, who had been praised by both parties, to replace him. But the Republican-led Senate refused to consider his nomination so that a new president could make the decision. Mr. Trump chose Neil M. Gorsuch to replace Justice Scalia, preserving the court's 5-to-4 split between conservatives and liberals.

In an interview in 2013, Justice Ginsburg said that she would not base her retirement plans on who was currently in the Oval Office. She said she would stay put "as long as I can do the job full steam, and that, at my age, is not predictable."

Earlier this year, Justice Anthony M. Kennedy, 81, announced his retirement. He had been a critical swing vote, generally voting with the court's conservatives but at times embracing liberal views in major cases.

Mr. Trump and Republican allies had hoped Justice Kennedy would step down so that a more conservative justice could be put in place while Senate Republicans were in the majority. Justice Kennedy was replaced by Justice Kavanaugh, one of his former clerks. The Kavanaugh nomination proceedings were the most contentious in decades, and the justice was confirmed in the closest Senate vote since the 19th century.

A hospital spokeswoman on Thursday directed questions about Justice Ginsburg's condition to the Supreme Court's press office.

LAWRENCE K. ALTMAN contributed reporting from New York, and ADAM LIPTAK from Washington.

Ruth Bader Ginsburg Undergoes Cancer Surgery

BY ADAM LIPTAK | DEC. 21, 2018

WASHINGTON — Justice Ruth Bader Ginsburg underwent surgery on Friday to remove two nodules from her left lung, according to Kathleen Arberg, a Supreme Court spokeswoman. The nodules were discovered during tests following a fall in November in which Justice Ginsburg fractured her ribs.

The surgery, a pulmonary lobectomy, took place at Memorial Sloan Kettering Cancer Center in New York City.

According to the justice's thoracic surgeon, Dr. Valerie W. Rusch, the nodules removed during surgery were found to be malignant, Ms. Arberg said in a statement.

After the surgery, she added, "there was no evidence of any remaining disease" and "scans performed before surgery indicated no evidence of disease elsewhere in the body."

"Currently, no further treatment is planned," Ms. Arberg said, "Justice Ginsburg is resting comfortably and is expected to remain in the hospital for a few days."

After such surgeries, medical experts said, some patients may experience difficulty breathing when exercising or walking distances.

Justice Ginsburg, 85, is the senior member of the court's four-member liberal wing. She has repeatedly vowed to stay on the court as long as her health holds and she stays mentally sharp. In a 2013 interview, she said she loved her work and intended to continue "as long as I can do the job full-steam, and that, at my age, is not predictable."

Justice Ginsburg has been treated for cancer twice before, attributing her survival partly to the medical care she received at the National Institutes of Health.

"Ever since my colorectal cancer in 1999, I have been followed by the N.I.H.," she said in the 2013 interview. "That was very lucky for me because they detected my pancreatic cancer at a very early stage" in 2009.

She has broken ribs twice, in 2012 and in November. In 2014, she underwent a heart procedure.

She has proved resilient in the aftermath of those episodes. After her most recent fall, she was back on the bench to hear arguments during the Supreme Court's two-week sitting that began on Nov. 26.

The new tumors could be primary lung cancers, meaning they originated in the lung. Or they could be growths that spread to her lung from cancer in another organ.

"When you have two lesions in the lung, it usually means it came from someplace else," said Dr. Raja Flores, chairman of thoracic surgery at the Icahn School of Medicine at Mount Sinai in Manhattan. "It's probably something that spread from the pancreas to the lungs."

That Justice Ginsburg is alive 10 years after being treated for pancreatic cancer — which is often rapidly fatal — indicates that she probably had a relatively slow-growing form of the disease. Therefore, Dr. Flores said, he expected that the tumors in her lungs would also tend to be slow-growing, what he calls "turtles."

Testing on the tissue removed during surgery will determine the diagnosis, he said.

Justice Ginsburg was born in Brooklyn in 1933, graduated from Cornell in 1954 and began law school at Harvard. After moving to New York with her husband, she transferred to Columbia, where she earned her law degree.

She taught at Rutgers and Columbia and was a leading courtroom advocate of women's rights before joining the court. As director of the Women's Rights Project of the American Civil Liberties Union in the 1970s, she brought a series of cases before the court that helped establish constitutional protections against sex discrimination.

Her litigation strategy invited comparison to that of Justice Thurgood Marshall, who was the architect of the civil rights movement's incremental legal attack on racial discrimination before he joined the court.

She was appointed to the court by President Bill Clinton in 1993. At the court these days, she moves slowly but asks sharp questions based on an assured command of the pertinent legal materials and factual record.

During the Obama administration, some liberals urged Justice Ginsburg to step down so that President Barack Obama could name her successor. She rejected the advice.

"I think it's going to be another Democratic president," Justice Ginsburg told The Washington Post in 2013. "The Democrats do fine in presidential elections; their problem is they can't get out the vote in the midterm elections."

President Trump, whose election proved her wrong, has been critical of Justice Ginsburg, saying in 2016 that "her mind is shot" and suggesting that she resign. His sharp words came after Justice Ginsburg criticized Mr. Trump in a series of interviews. She later said she had made a mistake in publicly commenting on a candidate and promised to be more "circumspect" in the future.

Justice Ginsburg was the subject of a recent documentary, and a dramatic film about her, "On the Basis of Sex," opens next week.

Mr. Trump has appointed two new members to the Supreme Court, Justices Neil M. Gorsuch and Brett M. Kavanaugh, moving it considerably to the right. Should he name Justice Ginsburg's replacement, Republican appointees would outnumber Democratic ones by a 6-to-3 margin.

LAWRENCE K. ALTMAN contributed reporting.

Ruth Bader Ginsburg Is Discharged From Hospital After Surgery

BY NIRAJ CHOKSHI | DEC. 26, 2018

JUSTICE RUTH BADER GINSBURG was discharged from the hospital on Tuesday and is recovering at home after undergoing surgery last week to remove two nodules from her left lung, according to Kathleen Arberg, a Supreme Court spokeswoman.

The malignant nodules, discovered in November after Justice Ginsburg fractured her ribs in a fall, were removed Friday at Memorial Sloan Kettering Cancer Center in New York City.

"There was no evidence of any remaining disease," Ms. Arberg said in a statement last week, citing Justice Ginsburg's thoracic surgeon, Dr. Valerie W. Rusch. "Scans performed before surgery indicated no evidence of disease elsewhere in the body."

Despite her hospitalization, Justice Ginsburg, 85, still participated in a Friday court vote preventing the Trump administration from immediately enforcing its new policy of denying asylum to migrants who illegally cross the Mexican border. She is the most senior member of the court's four-member liberal wing.

Justice Ginsburg has notably refused to allow health complications to get in the way of her work. She has been treated twice for cancer and, in a 2013 interview, said she would stay on the court "as long as I can do the job full steam."

In 2012, she broke two ribs without missing work. Two years later, she returned to work quickly after a heart procedure. Early last month, she fell at her office and went home. The following morning, a Thursday, she was hospitalized with three broken ribs from the fall. She was discharged the next day and worked from home.

Justice Ginsburg, who was appointed by President Bill Clinton in 1993, has become wildly popular among Democrats for her dogged defense of progressive ideals, including as a women's rights lawyer.

She has been given the affectionate nickname "Notorious R.B.G." and was the star of a well-received documentary this year. The actress Felicity Jones portrays her in "On the Basis of Sex," a movie released this week about her life.

Justice Ruth Bader Ginsburg Misses Supreme Court Arguments

BY ADAM LIPTAK | JAN. 7, 2019

WASHINGTON — Justice Ruth Bader Ginsburg, who underwent cancer surgery last month, was missing from the bench on Monday for the Supreme Court's first arguments since the court returned from its four-week holiday break.

Justice Ginsburg has suffered a number of health setbacks over the years but has never before missed an argument in her 25 years on the court.

Kathleen Arberg, a court spokeswoman, said Justice Ginsburg was working from home.

Chief Justice John G. Roberts Jr. announced his colleague's absence at the start of Monday's session, saying that "Justice Ginsburg is unable to be present today." He added that she would take part in the court's consideration of the day's two cases based on the briefs submitted by the parties and transcripts of the arguments.

Surgeons removed two nodules from Justice Ginsburg's left lung on Dec. 21. According to the justice's thoracic surgeon, Dr. Valerie W. Rusch, the nodules removed during surgery were found to be malignant, Ms. Arberg said at the time.

After the surgery, "there was no evidence of any remaining disease," Ms. Arberg said, adding: "Scans performed before surgery indicated no evidence of disease elsewhere in the body."

Justice Ginsburg, 85, is the senior member of the court's four-member liberal wing. President Trump has appointed two new members to the Supreme Court, Justices Neil M. Gorsuch and Brett M. Kavanaugh, moving it considerably to the right.

Should he name Justice Ginsburg's replacement, Republican appointees would outnumber Democratic ones six to three.

Justice Ginsburg has been treated for cancer twice before, attribut-

Justice Ruth Bader Ginsburg, during a portrait session for the Supreme Court on Nov. 30.

ing her survival partly to the medical care she received at the National Institutes of Health.

"Ever since my colorectal cancer in 1999, I have been followed by the N.I.H.," she said in the 2013 interview. "That was very lucky for me because they detected my pancreatic cancer at a very early stage" in 2009.

Doctors found the nodules removed last month during tests following a fall in November in which Justice Ginsburg fractured her ribs. She had broken her ribs once before, in 2012. In 2014, she underwent a heart procedure.

She did not miss any arguments after the earlier procedures. She was also on the bench in 2010 on the day after the death of her husband, Martin D. Ginsburg.

Justice Ginsburg has repeatedly vowed to stay on the court as long as her health holds and she stays mentally sharp. In 2013, she said she loved her work and intended to continue "as long as I can do the job full-steam, and that, at my age, is not predictable."

In 2004 and 2005, Chief Justice William H. Rehnquist missed many arguments during his treatment for thyroid cancer, though he continued to participate in the court's work. Chief Justice Rehnquist died in 2005.

Justice Ginsburg is revered in liberal circles, with her many fans calling her Notorious R.B.G., a nod to the rapper Notorious B.I.G. The justice has embraced the connection. "We were both born and bred in Brooklyn, New York," she likes to say.

She was born in 1933, graduated from Cornell in 1954 and began law school at Harvard. After moving to New York with her husband, she transferred to Columbia, where she earned her law degree.

She taught at Rutgers and Columbia and was a leading courtroom advocate of women's rights before joining the court. As director of the Women's Rights Project of the American Civil Liberties Union in the 1970s, she brought a series of cases before the court that helped establish constitutional protections against sex discrimination.

Her litigation strategy invited comparison to that of Justice Thurgood Marshall, who was the architect of the civil rights movement's incremental legal attack on racial discrimination before he joined the court.

Ruth Bader Ginsburg Is Cancer Free After Surgery, Supreme Court Says

BY ADAM LIPTAK | JAN. 11, 2019

WASHINGTON — Justice Ruth Bader Ginsburg is cancer free and on the mend after her recent surgery for the disease, a Supreme Court spokeswoman said on Friday.

"Her recovery from surgery is on track," the spokeswoman, Kathleen Arberg, said in a statement. "Post-surgery evaluation indicates no evidence of remaining disease, and no further treatment is required."

Justice Ginsburg, 85, underwent surgery in late December to remove two nodules from her left lung. She missed this week's arguments, and will be absent from the bench next week, too, Ms. Arberg said.

"Justice Ginsburg will continue to work from home next week and will participate in the consideration and decision of the cases on the basis of the briefs and the transcripts of oral arguments," Ms. Arberg said.

After next Wednesday's arguments, the court will take its four-week midwinter break, returning to the bench on Feb. 19.

CHAPTER 6

Screen, Stage and Pages

Considering the intense interest that many people have in Ginsburg, it is not surprising that she would be the subject of numerous books, films and stage productions. She's even become a pop culture meme as the "Notorious R.B.G.," with some fans even tattooing her face on their bodies. Ginsburg's legacy has left a lasting impression, and she continues to inspire men and women of all ages.

'Sisters in Law' Looks at Sandra Day O'Connor and Ruth Bader Ginsburg

REVIEW | BY LINDA GREENHOUSE | SEPT. 14, 2015

TWO YOUNG WOMEN, near age-mates, grow up in very different corners of the country, one in near isolation on a vast Southwestern cattle ranch and the other on the crowded streets of Brooklyn. They obtain superb educations, enter into early marriage and motherhood, and set out to make their way in a man's world. Decades later, we find them, having broken through more than a few glass ceilings, sitting together on the United States Supreme Court.

For anyone interested in the court, women's history or both, the story of Sandra Day O'Connor and Ruth Bader Ginsburg, their separate routes to the Supreme Court and what they accomplished during the more than 12 years they spent together is irresistible. But "Sisters in Law," with its ambitious subtitle, raises more questions than it answers. Did Justices O'Connor and Ginsburg really change the world? Or did they make it all the way to the Supreme Court, as the first and second women ever to serve there, because the world had changed?

There is a fascinating book struggling to emerge from the narrative structure Linda Hirshman has imposed on rich material. We glimpse it on those occasions when Hirshman chooses to highlight not the similarities between the two women but their differences. "Sandra Day O'Connor played defense; she would not permit the courts to roll the equality ball backward," we're told, while Ruth Ginsburg, for her part, "played offense." Another way to put it, perhaps, is that while Ginsburg set out to change the world for women through her advocacy and her skill at picking just the right case to bring to the court at the right time, O'Connor had no such ambition. She chose to live largely in the world that continually opened before her, as she turned her social networks to her advantage and found her way into electoral politics. (She became majority leader of the Arizona Senate, the first woman in the country to hold so high a state legislative office.) O'Connor's gift was the instinct for strategic and indispensable compromise. During her years at the center of the court — the role played since her departure in 2006 by Justice Anthony M. Kennedy — she often deployed concurring opinions "to make the conservative rulings more liberal and liberal opinions more conservative, usually by tying the outcome to the particular facts in the case."

"O'Connor was by no means a committed strategist for women's rights," Hirshman writes. "She was not a robust voice for social change." Hirshman, a lawyer and a scholar of feminism, whose last book was the well-received "Victory: The Triumphant Gay Revolution," writes with authority and obvious admiration about Ginsburg (although with an odd fixation on the justice's physical stature, describing her variously as "tiny," "minuscule," "skinny," "petite," "small" and, twice, "diminutive").

But Hirshman struggles noticeably with what to make of O'Connor ("large, blond," "open-faced, cheerful and energetic"), and with how to fit her into the book's overall construct. Hirshman properly cites O'Connor's "tightfisted votes for equality," her "ungenerous opinions even in cases where she voted for the woman's side" and her "endless dalliance with allowing ever more intrusive restrictions" on access to abortion. She expresses puzzlement at O'Connor's support for President Richard Nixon's nomination of a fellow Arizonan, William H. Rehnquist, to the Supreme Court in 1971. O'Connor's "passionate advocacy" for Rehnquist — she offered to testify for him at his confirmation hearing but was told that wouldn't be necessary — "presents the question of how serious a feminist she was." Really? Maybe O'Connor wasn't thinking in ideological terms at all, but was simply thrilled that her old friend, with whom she had shared top academic honors at Stanford Law School, had reached the pinnacle of the legal profession.

The book's title is offered without irony, but while Hirshman is too astute an observer to believe it fully, she is stuck with it nonetheless. This would have been a more coherent and satisfying book had she been willing to portray her subjects as I think she actually does understand them: not as sisters yoked together in a common project, but rather as representatives of the different ways that smart, ambitious women navigated life in mid-20th-century America, when social norms and expectations were changing but old patterns still prevailed.

Ginsburg, rejected for a clerkship by Justice Felix Frankfurter despite recommendations from leading law professors of the era because "I'm not hiring a woman," eventually committed herself to uprooting the legal system's built-in assumptions about the appropriate roles for women and men. O'Connor, offered a job as a legal secretary at a big California law firm because "our clients wouldn't

Associate Justices O'Connor and Ginsburg pose for a portrait in the Capitol's Statuary Hall, 2001.

stand for" being represented by a woman, has probably never to this day labeled herself a feminist. With one avenue blocked, she shifted course and made her way in private practice and government service.

But by the choices she made, O'Connor lived feminism as a fact even if she didn't embrace it as a cause, as Joan Biskupic documented in her sure-footed 2005 biography, "Sandra Day O'Connor: How the First Woman on the Supreme Court Became Its Most Influential Justice." Upon taking her seat on the court in September 1981 (three years almost to the day after "First Monday in October," a comedy that played the notion of a female Supreme Court justice for laughs, opened on Broadway), O'Connor became the ultimate symbol of women's progress. In retiring in January 2006, at the age of 75, to care for her Alzheimer's-disease-stricken husband, she became a symbol of women in a more traditional role, as caregiver. (While male justices have become widowers while serving on the court — Justice William J.

Brennan Jr. and Chief Justice Rehnquist are recent examples — none left the bench to care for their spouses.)

In the book's final pages, Hirshman suggests what might have been a powerful theme: that there had to be a Sandra Day O'Connor on the Supreme Court bench before there could be a Ruth Bader Ginsburg. "O'Connor had made it easier for her," Hirshman writes. She even seems to forgive O'Connor the failings she has spent many pages chronicling: "Sounding so conservative and framing her mildly pro-woman decisions time after time as protective of authority — employers, school administrators — she represented the farthest women could hope to go in light of the irresistible conservative resurgence of the late 20th and early 21st centuries." O'Connor displayed "laser judgment about what the court — and the society — would digest at any particular moment." Indeed, while Ruth Ginsburg's voice has become ever more powerful, it is, in the main, the power of the passionate and unanswerable dissent.

"Each one was better off for the other being there," Hirshman writes. And now there are three.

SISTERS IN LAW
How Sandra Day O'Connor and Ruth Bader Ginsburg Went to the Supreme Court and Changed the World
By Linda Hirshman
Illustrated. 390 pp. Harper. $28.99.

LINDA GREENHOUSE teaches at Yale Law School. Her new book (with Michael J. Graetz), "The Burger Court and the Rise of the Judicial Right," will be published next June.

'Notorious RBG: The Life and Times of Ruth Bader Ginsburg'

REVIEW | BY JENNIFER SENIOR | OCT. 25, 2015

AESTHETICALLY SPEAKING, "Notorious RBG: The Life and Times of Ruth Bader Ginsburg" is a cheery curio, as if a scrapbook and the Talmud decided to have a baby. Pages are filled with photographs of the Supreme Court justice old and young (ravishing, by the way). More entertaining are the dozens of images of her rendered in every conceivable medium — as nail art and shoulder tattoos, as needlepoint samplers and bronze busts, as surrealist watercolors, deadpan cartoons and somber illustrations. ("Fear the frill," says one, referring to her signature jabots.) Woven throughout are excerpts from Justice Ginsburg's most influential opinions, with added blocks of scholars' commentary strutting down the margins.

"Notorious RBG" began in 2013 as a saucy Tumblr blog by Shana Knizhnik, then a law student, shortly after the Supreme Court decided Shelby County v. Holder, which discarded a crucial provision of the Voting Rights Act. (For the hip-hop unlettered, Notorious RBG is a play on the Notorious B.I.G., the rapper who was murdered in 1997.) Justice Ginsburg read her dissent from the bench, which in the genteel, marbled universe of the Supreme Court, is most unusual — the equivalent of shaming your spouse in front of dinner guests. More unusual still was that she'd read two other dissents from the bench the day before.

Almost overnight, she became a supersignifier of liberal idealism, with Washington artist-activists plastering stickers and posters saying, "Can't Spell the Truth Without Ruth" all around town. A cottage industry of Ginsburgiana — greeting cards, T-shirts, homemade Halloween costumes ("Ruth Baby Ginsburg," in the case of toddlers) — was born, and Ms. Knizhnik's Tumblr became a clearinghouse for it. Objets de Ruth are now part of the temple of highbrow kitsch, along with Freud bobblehead dolls and Shakespeare rubber ducks.

Though Ms. Knizhnik collaborated on the research and reporting of "Notorious RBG," it's her co-author, Irin Carmon, an MSNBC journalist known for her smarts and feminist bona fides, who wrote the book and gives it its distinctive voice. (Ms. Knizhnik also curated the images, naturally; and checked the facts.) As Ms. Carmon explains in a prefatory author's note, she and Ms. Knizhnik are both "#millennials," which some readers may take as an early typographical cue to close the book and slowly back away.

This book is not for them. "Notorious RBG" may be a playful project, but it asks to be read seriously. It's an artisanal hagiography, a frank and admiring piece of fan nonfiction. One chapter is devoted almost entirely to Justice Ginsburg's workout (impressive) and lace collars (she owns at least a dozen). Early on, we learn that Justice Ginsburg was a fan of Nancy Drew as a child, and "Notorious RBG," with its earnest superhero framing, reads like a Nancy Drew novel itself: "After years of toil, often in the shadows, she is poised to explain to the country just what is going wrong." It's an Honest Abe tale for the 20-something set.

Justice Ginsburg's story of self-invention is pretty remarkable. At Harvard Law, she was one of just nine women, and she didn't have access to one of the reading rooms. (Never mind that she was a member of the law review.) She was refused a clerkship with Justice Felix Frankfurter in part because she was a mother, in part because he liked to curse and didn't wish to watch his language. When she argued her first case before the Supreme Court, Justice Harry Blackmun rated her a C+ in his diary. ("Very precise female," he wrote.)

To this female book critic, who will hand in her review to a female editor, who in turn reports to another female editor, this cold universe of belittlement is unimaginable. That I responded so personally to it is a testimony to Ms. Carmon's storytelling and panache. I was especially moved by the chapter about Justice Ginsburg's husband, Marty Ginsburg, which confirmed Sheryl Sandberg's dictum, "The most important career choice you'll make is who you marry." Mr. Ginsburg cooked for Justice Ginsburg, made professional sacrifices for her, and at one point proclaimed, "I think that the most important thing I have done is enable Ruth to do what she has done."

Read his note to her 10 days before he died. I dare you not to cry.

This book is also a direct descendant of contemporary feminist websites (Ms. Carmon spent two years as a staff writer at Jezebel) and as such, has not just their strengths — wit, sharp consciousness-raising — but also, on occasion, their weaknesses (a Manichaean worldview, a lack of tonal maturity).

I am not sure this book's target audience will much care. Nor, I'm guessing, will this audience care that the book doesn't wade too deeply into the marshes of Justice Ginsburg's jurisprudence. Ms. Carmon does a fine job of showing how shrewd Justice Ginsburg was as a women's rights lawyer, deliberately taking on male plaintiffs who had been disenfranchised in their caregiver roles. Through a discreet back door, she established a meaningful body of law that said neither men's nor women's rights should be determined or limited by sex.

But Justice Ginsburg always insisted that progress should come in slow, methodical steps rather than extreme gestures. In 1993, she gave a famous (one might say notorious) lecture that decried Roe v. Wade because the decision "invited no dialogue with legislators," but wiped out, in a single stroke, every state's abortion law.

Ms. Carmon mentions this lecture. But as the book winds down, she does not so much as remark upon — much less reckon with — the idea that Justice Ginsburg's belief in incrementalism might live in tension with her recent votes on marriage equality, which invalidated many state laws and made no overtures to state legislatures at all. Yet these votes clearly suggest that she sometimes does see a role for the courts as an agent of transformative social change.

Perhaps Justice Ginsburg thought the country was ready for marriage equality. Perhaps she saw these landmark same-sex marriage cases as legally different from Roe v. Wade — as two instances of the law providing a clear answer, rather than begging for discretion. For now, we cannot say.

There is much about Justice Ginsburg that remains enigmatic. The achievement of "Notorious RBG" is that the authors make this unassuming, most studious woman come pulsing to life. A colleague of the justice's once said, "The anecdote that describes her best is that there are no anecdotes." In this way, Justice Ginsburg is a bit like the Mona Lisa, whose likeness has also launched a thousand fanciful appropriations. To be a scrim for the world's projections, it helps to be a little hard to read.

Notorious RBG
The Life and Times of Ruth Bader Ginsburg
By Irin Carmon and Shana Knizhnik
Illustrated. 227 pages. Dey St. $19.99.

Justice Ruth Bader Ginsburg Presides Over Shylock's Appeal

BY RACHEL DONADIO | JULY 27, 2016

VENICE — What do Supreme Court justices do on their summer vacations? For Justice Ruth Bader Ginsburg — longtime liberal standardbearer, recent Donald J. Trump critic — this year's answer is: Go to Venice, watch your grandson perform in a production of "The Merchant of Venice" and preside over a mock appeal of the city's most notorious resident, Shylock.

And so, on Wednesday afternoon, in the monumental 16th-century Scuola Grande di San Rocco, beneath ceiling paintings by Tintoretto, Justice Ginsburg and four other judges, including the United States ambassador to Italy, John R. Phillips, heard arguments on behalf of Shylock and two other characters, before reaching a unanimous ruling.

"I'd describe it as fun," Justice Ginsburg said of the coming mock appeal in an interview on Tuesday, in which she talked about Venice, which she first visited on her honeymoon in 1954, and Shakespeare, whose work she loves — but not about Mr. Trump, weeks after she said she regretted her remarks criticizing the man who is now the Republican presidential nominee.

The mock appeal began where the play ended: Shylock, the conniving Venetian Jewish moneylender, insists on collecting a pound of flesh from Antonio, who has defaulted on a loan. But a lawyer, actually Portia disguised as a man, finds Shylock guilty of conspiring against Antonio and rules that he must hand over half his property to Antonio and the other half to the state.

Antonio says he will forgo his half, on the condition that Shylock convert to Christianity and will his estate to Jessica, Shylock's wicked and rebellious daughter, who has run off to Genoa with Lorenzo, a Christian. Shylock, humiliated, agrees.

After about two hours of arguments and about 20 minutes of deliberations, the judges issued a unanimous ruling: To remove the question of the pound of flesh — "We agreed it was a merry sport, and no court would enforce it," Justice Ginsburg said — to restore Shylock's property, to restore the 3,000 ducats that he had lent to Antonio, and to nullify the demand of his conversion.

"The conversion was sought by Antonio," Justice Ginsburg said. "The defendant in the case was decreeing the sanction. I never heard of a defendant in any system turning into a judge as Antonio did." She added, to laughter, "And finally, after four centuries of delay in seeking payment, we think that Shylock is out of time in asking for interest."

The court was not unanimous in what to do with Portia. The judges ruled that because Portia was "an impostor," a "hypocrite" and "a trickster," she would be sanctioned by having to attend law school at the University of Padua, where one of the judges, Laura Picchio Forlati, taught. Then she would have to pursue a master of laws degree at Wake Forest University, where another of the judges, Richard Schneider, is a professor and dean.

Mr. Schneider said it wasn't daunting to share the bench with Justice Ginsburg. "Because she was wonderful and welcoming," he said.

The audience was gripped, even in sweltering heat. "It's an intellectual version of reality television," said Dominic Green, a Shakespeare scholar and professor at Boston College, who attended.

It was an all-star Shakespeare event. Before deliberations began, F. Murray Abraham recited the "hath not a Jew eyes?" speech. While the judges deliberated, the Shakespeare scholars Stephen Greenblatt and James Shapiro discussed the play.

The mock appeal was linked to a production of "The Merchant of Venice" being staged in the main square of Venice's Jewish ghetto, performed by the New York-based Compagnia de' Colombari, part of a series of events this year marking the ghetto's 500th anniversary.

Justice Ginsburg said she'd become involved in the mock appeal after learning about the "Merchant of Venice" production from

Justice Ginsburg and her fellow jurists before contemplating Shylock's fate. The mock appeal began where the play ends.

friends who spend time each year in Venice, including Judith Martin, who writes as Miss Manners, and the mystery novelist Donna Leon. (Asked who had paid for her visit, the justice said she had come to Venice after speaking at a conference hosted by New York University in Barcelona.)

Over the years, Justice Ginsburg has presided over several other mock Shakespeare appeals. "In the one I like most, the question was whether Hamlet was competent to stand trial for the murder of Polonius," Justice Ginsburg said. "My judgment was, yes he was. But not only Polonius, but the grand jury should consider whether he should be indicted for Ophelia's death."

After Justice Ginsburg expressed interest in a mock appeal, the play's director, Karin Coonrad, did a Skype audition with the justice's grandson, Paul Spera, an actor who lives in Paris. She cast him as Lorenzo, who runs away with Jessica, Shylock's daughter.

"He's very, very good," Justice Ginsburg said of her grandson's performance. "I admit to being a little prejudiced on the subject, but I thought he was wonderful."

Mr. Spera, 30, said his grandmother had noticed that they had cut two lines from a famous scene with the refrain "In such a night as this." "My bubbe was a little disappointed by that," Mr. Spera said after opening night. Yes, he said, he calls her "bubbe," the Yiddish term for grandmother.

There had been some controversy among Jews in Venice about performing such a problematic play. "When I was going to school, 'The Merchant of Venice' was banned because it was known as an anti-Semitic play," Justice Ginsburg said. She said she agreed with the assessment. "That's what Shakespeare meant it to be," she said. "Shylock is a villain. He's insisting on a pound of flesh. He's sharpening his knife."

Shaul Bassi, a professor of Shakespeare at the University of Venice and a key organizer of the mock trial and the play, sees it differently. "It's not an anti-Semitic play, it's a play about anti-Semitism," he said. Mr. Bassi, a co-founder of the nonprofit organization Beit Venezia, said he hoped the production would show the ghetto as a meeting place of cultures. "This is an incredible opportunity to rethink this place," he said.

The Jewish community of Venice, which numbers 450 people, is raising funds to restore the five synagogue buildings on the ghetto's main square, which are crumbling after lack of maintenance, and to reimagine the Jewish Museum. "It's not a mausoleum, it's not a look at the past," said David Landau, who leads the community's restoration committee.

Back at the mock trial, after the judges wrapped up, the last word didn't go to Justice Ginsburg but to Arrigo Cipriani, the owner of Harry's Bar, which sponsored a cocktail reception after the ruling. Justice Ginsburg entered to applause, and was promptly handed a Bellini.

In 'RBG,' the Life and Times of a Beloved and Controversial Supreme Court Justice

REVIEW | BY A.O. SCOTT | MAY 3, 2018

RUTH BADER GINSBURG was the second woman appointed to the United States Supreme Court, but she's probably the first justice to become a full-fledged pop-cultural phenomenon. "RBG," a loving and informative documentary portrait of Justice Ginsburg during her 85th year on earth and her 25th on the bench, is both evidence of this status and a partial explanation of how it came about.

Directed by Betsy West and Julie Cohen, the film is a jaunty assemblage of interviews, public appearances and archival material, organized to illuminate its subject's temperament and her accomplishments so far. Though it begins with audio snippets of Justice Ginsburg's right-wing detractors — who see her as a "demon," a "devil" and a threat to America — "RBG" takes a pointedly high road through recent political controversies. Its celebration of Justice Ginsburg's record of progressive activism and jurisprudence is partisan but not especially polemical. The filmmakers share her convictions and assume that the audience will, too.

Which might be true, and not only because much of the audience is likely to consist of liberals. Before she was named to the federal bench by Jimmy Carter in 1980, the future justice had argued a handful of important sex-discrimination cases in front of the Supreme Court. What linked these cases — she won five out of six — was the theory that the equal protection clause of the 14th Amendment should apply to women and could be used to remedy discrepancies in hiring, business practices and public policy.

The idea that women are equal citizens — that barring them from certain jobs and educational opportunities and treating them as the social inferiors of men are unfair — may not seem especially controversial now. "RBG" uses Justice Ginsburg's own experiences to emphasize how different things were not so long ago. At Harvard Law School, she was one of nine women in a class of hundreds, and was asked by the dean (as all the women were) why she thought she deserved to take what should have been a man's place.

The biographical part of "RBG" tells a story that is both typical and exceptional. It's a reminder that the upward striving of first- and second-generation Jewish immigrants in the middle decades of the 20th century was accompanied by fervent political idealism. Justice Ginsburg's career was marked by intense intellectual ambition and also by a determination to use the law as an instrument of change.

The film also chronicles her marriage to Martin Ginsburg. They met as undergraduates at Cornell, and for the next 63 years, Mr. Ginsburg (who died in 2010) was his wife's tireless supporter and champion, a man whose commitment to domestic egalitarianism was extraordinary in his time and far from common today. As their friends and children explain — and as Mr. Ginsburg, a New York tax lawyer, often said himself — he was responsible for cooking meals and cracking jokes while she was making history. He also, when Byron White retired from the Supreme Court, made sure that her name was high on President Clinton's list of candidates.

It would be fascinating to learn more about that campaign, and also to have a finer-grained sense of the institutional and interpersonal dynamics of the court over the past quarter-century. But "RBG" reasonably chooses to focus on Justice Ginsburg herself, and relishes every moment of her company. It also shows why she has become such an inspiration for younger feminists, like Irin Carmon and Shana Knizhnik, whose 2015 book "Notorious RBG: The Life and Times of Ruth Bader Ginsburg" helped created the contemporary image of a fierce, uncompromising and gracious champion of women's rights.

That those rights are in a new phase of embattlement goes without saying. The movie's touch is light and its spirit buoyant, but there is no mistaking its seriousness or its passion. Those qualities resonate powerfully in the dissents that may prove to be Justice Ginsburg's most enduring legacy, and "RBG" is, above all, a tribute to her voice.

Ninja Supreme Court Justice: Ruth Bader Ginsburg Has Fun With Fame

BY MELENA RYZIK | MAY 9, 2018

The star of the documentary "RBG" has embraced her popularity as another tool in her effort to help women advance.

WASHINGTON — No one knew when, or even how or where, Ruth Bader Ginsburg would pop up. The Supreme Court justice was due at a screening here of "RBG," a new documentary chronicling her exemplary life. But she was not tied to the night's tightly scripted schedule — at some point she would just appear, "like a ninja," an organizer said.

Gathered in a theater at the Naval Heritage Center, the crowd was amped. There were lawmakers (progressive Democrats and a smattering of conservatives); the justice's family, friends and former law clerks; her colleague Justice Stephen Breyer; and self-described fan girls and boys.

"I just love how she takes no crap from anybody," said Kerri Sheehan, a 49-year-old video producer, who wore a T-shirt printed, Warhol-style, with the justice's face. "There's no sugarcoating."

When the justice arrived, bodyguards encircling her, the audience gave her a standing ovation, then hushed until she claimed her seat. She wore her hair pulled back with one of her beloved scrunchies, in navy velvet; a maroon tweedy blazer; slate-blue belled slacks; jewelry in just about every possible place jewelry can go; and carried her own large handbag. In front of her, arms shot up for the stealth selfie-with-a-famous-person snap. She didn't mind.

Justice Ginsburg is an unlikely celebrity but then again, we live in an age full of those. What makes her ascendance to pop culture icon — the Notorious RBG, y'all — truly surprising is that, at 85, she is having fun with her unexpected fame, and making careful and inspired use of it for her own savvy ends.

"Ruth was so far ahead of her time that she was alone for decades," Gloria Steinem wrote in an email, listing the ways her friend and feminist compatriot of nearly half a century has been at the forefront of cultural shifts. "Ruth acted on the intertwining of racism and sexism long before it was called intersectionality. And she was principled in her own field," the law, even though, as a woman, she was not initially welcome in its highest ranks.

"I can't tell you how happy it makes me to see her name on campus T-shirts as the Notorious RBG," Ms. Steinem added. "A majority consciousness is finally catching up to where she's been all along."

Theodore B. Olson, the conservative lawyer and a longtime friend of Justice Ginsburg (he also argued Bush v. Gore, representing George W. Bush, in front of her), has seen her evolve into an idol.

"She knows the fact that she's doing this, and embracing it, means so much to young women — because she's teaching, every time she gives a speech or talks to people," he said after the screening. "And that's what this movie will do too. So she knows how valuable it is."

Mr. Olson calls her a warrior. Ms. Steinem, in the documentary, calls her a superhero. (Marvel agrees: in "Deadpool 2," when the title character is assembling his X Force, he flicks through a photo of her as a candidate.)

For Julie Cohen and Betsy West, the directors of "RBG," she was, first off, a hard-to-wrangle subject. Each had interviewed her for other projects, but when they approached her about the documentary she told them she wouldn't talk to them for at least two years. She was 82 at the time.

They persisted, interviewing colleagues and clients for whom she did landmark work. Eventually they were granted an audience with her, trailing along on family vacations, to the opera, and on a visit with her granddaughter, a recent Harvard Law graduate who calls her Bubbie. In her chambers, Justice Ginsburg traced her path from law school, where the dean asked her and the eight other female students (in a class of about 500) how they could justify taking the place of a man. Though she made the law review and graduated at the top of her class at Columbia, no firm would hire her, a Jewish woman and already a mother; she became a professor instead. If she felt any frustration at being shortchanged professionally, it didn't erupt. "Reacting in anger or annoyance will not advance one's ability to persuade," she wrote in her 2016 autobiography, "My Own Words."

But a certain feistiness has become part of her public image. It's in her withering dissents, each practically a social media event, and in Kate McKinnon's frisky impression of her on "Saturday Night Live." The likeness was not uncanny, she told the documentary directors, but she enjoyed it anyway.

Justice Ginsburg did not see "RBG" until its premiere at Sundance in January. "She laughed and she pulled out her handkerchief three times and dabbed her eyes," Ms. West reported. She watched it again in Washington, sitting next to her daughter, Jane C. Ginsburg, a professor at Columbia Law School, but did not linger at the reception. A night owl who sometimes still pores over cases at 3 a.m., she may well have been going home to work. She catches up on sleep on weekends: the directors once arrived at her Watergate apartment on a Saturday afternoon to find her padding about in vintage loungewear, sipping the day's first coffee.

She is still sparing with interviews — she declined to comment for this article — but encouraged her personal trainer, Bryant Johnson, to write a book, "The RBG Workout," which features illustrations of her doing planks and push-ups.

Now, her "RBG" notoriety may only grow. (The nickname is a play on the Notorious B.I.G., the rapper — a fellow Brooklynite, as she likes to point out.) There is also a feature about her in the works, with Felicity Jones playing her as a young lawyer, and Armie Hammer as her doting husband, Martin Ginsburg. The justice makes a cameo, as herself.

It is the kind of attention that eluded her when she made her groundbreaking strides, helping to create the legal framework for women's rights in the 1970s. As a lawyer with the American Civil Liberties

Union, she won five of the six cases she argued before the Supreme Court, maintaining that the 14th Amendment's equal protection clause should apply to issues of gender discrimination.

"These are just stories that weren't being told," Ms. Cohen said of the current focus on Justice Ginsburg's pioneering career. "It's part of this unearthing and rethinking of parts of our history that we've all been ignoring for so long."

Ted W. Lieu, a Democratic congressman from California who attended the Washington screening, was among those astonished by her accomplishments. "I'm a lawyer, and I didn't know" about her track record, he said. "You would know some of the cases, but you never knew who argued it, or knew the strategy."

One notion threaded through the documentary is that the diminutive Justice Ginsburg is not the usual vision of authority. Friends and colleagues remark that she is quiet, reserved — not at all what is traditionally thought of as powerful.

"She just has an unusual degree of confidence for a woman of her era," Ms. Cohen said. "There is a way to have a commanding presence even if you're small and quiet, which I think is a good lesson for women."

To Harryette Gordon Helsel, who has been friends with Kiki, as she calls Justice Ginsburg, since they were in kindergarten, the dynamo in "RBG" felt familiar, the same person who introduced a teenage Ms. Helsel to a fellow who wanted a blind date. (In August the Helsels will have been married for 65 years.)

Justice Ginsburg's collegiality and capacity for friendship are striking. Mr. Olson, the conservative lawyer, recalled New Year's Eve parties at her home with Martin Ginsburg, when the guest list included Justice Antonin Scalia and his wife. The Champagne flowed early, and for the midnight meal, Mr. Ginsburg would cook something Justice Scalia had hunted.

"Nino would go some place like Arkansas and kill wild boar, and Marty was a real consummate chef," Mr. Olson recalled. "He must've had something like 400 cookbooks. Ruth really didn't even know where the kitchen was." The justices, ideological opposites but close pals, sat next to each other at the short end of the table. (Mr. Ginsburg, a lawyer and an extraordinary champion of his wife for a man of his generation, died in 2010. Justice Scalia died in 2016.)

One person Justice Ginsburg now relies on is Mr. Johnson, her trainer. They've been working together since 1999, after her first bout with cancer. After a diagnosis of pancreatic cancer in 2009, "she said, when can we start back?' " Mr. Johnson recalled. They meet several times a week for hourlong sessions, which have become the stuff of Washington lore. Stephen Colbert sputtered alongside recently as the justice, wearing a T-shirt that read "Super Diva!" silently went through her routine.

"The whole time that I've trained the justice, the one word she has never used with me is 'can't,' " Mr. Johnson said. "Even when I told her we were going to do push-ups — she looked me with a side-eye, like maybe I was locked on stupid and stuck on dumb. But she didn't say anything. And when Justice Ginsburg finally did push-ups off her knees, she lit up."

The day Mr. Colbert joined her, she did more than 30 push-ups, Mr. Johnson said, and was disappointed the clip didn't show more of her one-legged planks. "I tell people that she's tough as nails," he said. "She is just consistently doing what has to be done, and exercise is one of those things. Just do the right thing, at all costs. And that's just so inspiring."

For those wondering about her longevity, the directors of "RBG" say they were impressed by her verve and intellectual sharpness. "It's almost like she gives you the feeling that she's going to be around on the court, because that's her plan," Ms. Cohen said. Justice Ginsburg has already hired law clerks through 2020. "Our experience going through this process is, if she says she's going to do something, she does it," Ms. Cohen said.

From Top Law School Grad to Notorious R.B.G.: The Evolution of a Supreme Court Justice

REVIEW | BY LINDA GREENHOUSE | OCT. 29, 2018

RUTH BADER GINSBURG
A Life
By Jane Sherron De Hart
Illustrated. 723 pp. Alfred A. Knopf. $35.

DURING AN ONSTAGE INTERVIEW this summer following a performance in New York of a play about her late friend Antonin Scalia, Ruth Bader Ginsburg, a.k.a. Notorious R.B.G., then a few months past her 85th birthday, observed offhandedly: "I consider myself a flaming feminist."

Decades earlier, as a 21-year-old newly married Army wife, she applied for a job as a claims examiner in a Social Security office near her husband's post in Lawton, Okla. The position carried the respectable Civil Service rank of GS-5. But when she informed the personnel office that she was pregnant, she was offered a clerk-typist job at the lowly rank of GS-2. A pregnant woman would be unable to travel for the necessary claims examiner training, a bureaucrat explained, adding that, by the way, once she had the baby she would have to quit the job altogether.

Did the future flaming feminist protest, demand justice or otherwise stand up for herself in the face of such manifest unfairness? No, she did not, Jane Sherron De Hart informs us in "Ruth Bader Ginsburg," the first full biography of the second woman to serve on the Supreme Court. Ginsburg needed the job and "rationalized the incident as 'just the way things are.'"

A lot has happened in the intervening 64 years to make the way things were appear so outlandish as to be scarcely believable to the young women who have turned Ruth Ginsburg into a matriarchal icon, surely one of the culture's most unlikely rock stars. Was she really one of only nine women out of 552 students in her Harvard Law School class of 1959? Can it be true that, tied for first in her class at Columbia Law School (to which she transferred in her final year, in order to be with her husband in New York City), she couldn't find a job after graduation? When she began her teaching career in 1963, were there really only 18 female tenured law professors in the entire country? Believe it, millennials.

The journey from then to now, in society in general and law in particular, is well documented. And Ginsburg's role in the law-related aspects of that transformation will be familiar, at least in general terms, to anyone drawn to this weighty book (546 pages of text and 111 pages of endnotes, to say nothing of the bibliography and index). Readers will know of the young lawyer's pathbreaking (or, as she might put it, "way paving") litigation campaign that persuaded the nine men of the Supreme Court, step by tentative step, to create an entirely new jurisprudence of sex equality.

The question for any Ginsburg biography — and there will be others, including a long-anticipated authorized one by Wendy Williams and Mary Hartnett of Georgetown Law School, still some years down the road — is not only what happened, but why. Why Ruth Ginsburg? Why this quiet woman whose conversation was marked by long awkward pauses, whose academic passion was for civil procedure and who "never had the slightest intention of becoming an expert on discrimination law and equal protection analysis"? The young women who hang on her every dissenting opinion and who tattoo her image, complete with lace jabot, onto their arms may be tempted to reduce her life's trajectory to a tale of "don't get mad, get even," but as this book amply demonstrates, it's a good deal more elusive than that.

We can quickly discount Ginsburg's own often-repeated claim that "it was all a matter of being in the right place at the right time." De Hart, a scholar of women's history and an emeritus professor at the University of California, Santa Barbara, searches doggedly for an alternative explanation: "Adopting a feminist identity is a process — one in which her own life experience intersected with a larger historical canvas colored by the past and stretching well beyond the United States."

That's a framing of the mystery, not its solution. Part of the answer clearly lay with Ginsburg's mother, Celia Amster Bader, the Brooklyn household's center of gravity, who had given up her own ambitions years earlier in order to help put her brother through Cornell. Before she died, two days before Ruth's high school graduation, she had transferred those ambitions to a daughter who excelled on her own route to Cornell.

Another clue to the mystery lay in the fortuity of a two-year job Ginsburg accepted, early in her career, to write a book about the Swedish legal system, part of a new Project on International Procedure at Columbia Law School (where she would later become the first female full professor). She found life in Sweden eye-opening, particularly the assumption that there was nothing unusual or untoward about women combining work and family obligations. Child care was effortlessly available. An article by the editor of a feminist magazine was a hot topic in Swedish academic circles. "We ought to stop harping on the concept of 'women's two roles,' " the editor, Eva Moberg, had written. "Both men and women have one principal role, that of being people."

It wouldn't be an exaggeration to say, although De Hart doesn't quite lock this piece into place, that converting this observation into reality became Ruth Ginsburg's lifework. First as an advocate and later as a justice, she made it her goal to dismantle the structures that embody "overbroad generalizations about the way men and women are," as she put it in a majority opinion just last year.

And finally, surely, there was her marriage to Martin Ginsburg, a man far ahead of his time, or of any time for that matter. Viewers of "RBG," the surprise movie hit of the summer, glimpsed the quality of the 56-year marriage that ended with Marty Ginsburg's death in 2010. It was a true partnership, a daily reminder of what equality of the sexes could be.

The charming fact that Marty did the cooking was only the tip of a much more consequential iceberg. A hugely successful tax lawyer, his own ego intact, he reveled in his wife's accomplishment and dedicated himself to helping her achieve her ambition to become a judge. This prize did not fall into her lap. President Jimmy Carter passed her over three times before finally naming her to the federal appeals court in Washington, D.C., in the waning months of his administration. President Bill Clinton needed more persuading than is commonly realized, owing in part to the fact that the feminist leaders who came later to lionize Justice Ginsburg mistrusted her voting record on the appeals court, where she often sided with the conservatives. "The women are against her," Clinton grumbled to Senator Daniel Patrick Moynihan, a key champion of her candidacy for the vacancy created by Justice Byron R. White's retirement in 1993.

De Hart's lengthy narrative, strong on facts, is less so on analysis. (And her grip on Supreme Court procedure is shaky: The court, for example, does not have a "spring term.") We are left to wonder what it was, beyond obvious dismay at the court's conservative turn, that transformed a judge known for singing the virtues of minimalism and consensus-building into a famous dissenter, the heroine of a recent book for young readers titled "I Dissent: Ruth Bader Ginsburg Makes Her Mark." "She has objected. She has resisted. She has dissented," the text reads. "Disagreeable? No. Determined? Yes. This is how Ruth Bader Ginsburg changed her life — and ours." It's almost as if, were we not lucky enough to have Ruth Bader Ginsburg among us in this troubled time, we would have had to invent her. Icons, it seems, are made as well as born.

LINDA GREENHOUSE, who teaches at Yale Law School, covered the Supreme Court for The Times for three decades. Her latest book is a memoir, "Just a Journalist: On the Press, Life, and the Spaces Between."

Bringing to Life the Ruth Bader Ginsburg Only Her Family Knows

BY MELENA RYZIK | DEC. 27, 2018

DANIEL STIEPLEMAN WAS SITTING at his Uncle Martin's funeral in 2010, when he heard a eulogy that sparked a screenplay. The story had to do with a case that his uncle, a tax lawyer, tried with his wife, who happened to be Ruth Bader Ginsburg.

It was the only case the couple worked together, and it encapsulated, Stiepleman thought, so much about the era and their marriage: the discrimination that women faced; the path his aunt blazed, as she won cases to counter that discrimination even before she became a Supreme Court justice; and the unusually equal partnership she had with Martin Ginsburg, in the courtroom and at home.

In 2011, Stiepleman, a fledgling screenwriter, called his aunt — who was not yet the pop culture phenom known as Notorious RBG — to pitch her on doing a movie about her life. "I said, I have this idea, I would love your permission and I would really love your help," he recalled. "And there was this pause and she said, 'Well, if that's how you think you'd like to spend your time.'"

In the seven years between that call and the new film, "On the Basis of Sex," the production became another point of connection for the extended Ginsburg clan. Even for a biopic, this one is unusually family-oriented: It traces Justice Ginsburg's extraordinary relationships as much as her unparalleled career.

She opened her files in the Library of Congress to her nephew, who found inspiration in the snarky comments she made in the margins of briefs. She reviewed several drafts of the script, as did her daughter, Jane C. Ginsburg, whose childhood and teenage years are depicted onscreen. Jane's son, Paul Spera, an actor, has a small part. And Stiepleman, whose mother, Claire, and Martin Ginsburg were siblings, is also an executive producer, "which basically means I'm the Ruth-whisperer," he said.

Their closeness, which blossomed during filmmaking, was imperative. "There wasn't going to be a movie, at least not by him, if my mother wasn't comfortable with it," Jane Ginsburg said.

Having so many family members participate, and the approval of the justice herself — she even makes a cameo — gave the movie an air of indispensable authenticity, said Mimi Leder, the director. Ginsburg reviewed the script as if it were a contract. "Like any good lawyer, she doesn't leave any detail untrammeled," said Felicity Jones, who plays her.

The objections started with the very first line, which described young Ruth wearing heels to her orientation at Harvard Law School; she wore flats, she explained to her nephew, because she walked to campus. He persuaded her to let the fancier footwear stay — just about the only argument he won.

Beyond giving Jones's casting her blessing, it was also "very important to her who played Marty," Leder said.

He was tall, fair-haired in his youth with a chiseled jawline, a charismatic storyteller who never missed a punch line. Armie Hammer fit the bill. When the stars went to Justice Ginsburg's chambers to meet her, "she couldn't take her eyes off Armie," Jones said.

To get her portrayal right, Jones, the British actress and star of "Rogue One: A Star Wars Story," studied audiotapes from Ginsburg's early lawsuits, divining that her Brooklyn accent became more pronounced as she grew more impassioned. They spent time together at the justice's home, where, Jones said, "she very proudly showed me her incredibly tidy desk," which is near her bed. (She still keeps a night owl's working hours, with phone meetings about the script starting at 11 p.m., after she'd finished her typically long day at court.)

Being in her orbit emboldened Jones. "Every time I sort of feel overwhelmed by something, I constantly come back to her," she said. "I think, how would she have dealt with this situation and navigated it? After playing Ruth, I realized how important it is to have a voice in the world and to express that. If she wasn't scared to do it, I shouldn't be."

The film is an origin story, revealing how a young mother went from one of the few women in her class at Harvard to an architect of the laws that overturned gender discrimination (no more bias "on the basis of sex"). The 1970s case that the Ginsburgs fought together, Moritz v. Commissioner of Internal Revenue — which Martin brought to his wife, then a law professor — was the first time she delivered oral arguments in court. In a real-life twist that was, Stiepleman said, "a gift from the screenplay gods," the opposing counsel was overseen by the couple's former Harvard Law dean, who had been less than kind to his female students, asking them what qualified them to take the place of men.

Of course, the story was also Hollywoodized. That pivotal moment when Ruth freezes in court and cedes the floor to her husband? "There's not a shred of truth to that," her daughter said, a point the justice has also made. "I didn't stumble," she said in a recent Q. and A. after a screening in Manhattan, where the audience included Gloria Steinem and Hillary Clinton.

The mid-December event was held before Ginsburg had surgery to remove cancerous nodules from her lungs. But her health was still a fresh concern, since she broke three ribs last month. In a conversation with the NPR correspondent Nina Totenberg, she assured the crowd she was feeling "better each week" and was back to her regular, strenuous workouts with her trainer. "Even planks," she said.

If she didn't seek out the biopic, she seemed to appreciate it. "The film is part fact, part imaginative," she said that night. "But what's wonderful about it is that the imaginative parts fit in with the story so well." (In lieu of interviews, Ginsburg participated in several Q. and A.s.)

Some of the legal groundwork may be familiar, thanks to the wildly popular documentary "RBG," released in May. (Among her many firsts, Ginsburg is the only sitting Supreme Court justice to be the subject of two films in the same year.) But the revelation of the feature is in its focus on her home life: her terrible cooking, devoted mothering and spats with the teenage Jane, as well as the way in which Martin Ginsburg stepped up as parent and household co-leader.

Stiepleman viewed his uncle as an exemplary husband and father, a role model, and hoped to convey that onscreen. "It was that dynamic of two people my age, trying to figure out how to live at home what they're also fighting for in court, which is true equality," he said.

"This movie is as much about their love story as about how change happens," Leder said.

For the Ginsburg family, seeing their life recreated onscreen, detailed down to the jewelry Ruth Bader Ginsburg wore when she argued before the Supreme Court, was surreal, "a step out of reality," Jane Ginsburg said.

The movie presents the teenage Jane as brash and opinionated (a characterization also based in part on Jane's daughter, Clara Spera, Stiepleman said). And though in real life, the young Jane was politically and socially engaged, with a consciousness-raising group and an internship at Ms. magazine, she does not believe she led her mother

The justice's nephew, the screenwriter Daniel Stiepleman, left, and her daughter, Jane C. Ginsburg, who said, "There wasn't going to be a movie, at least not by him, if my mother wasn't comfortable with it."

into a more forcefully feminist outlook, as the film suggests. "I think my mother had a much greater tolerance for poetic license than I did," she said.

The future justice was a stickler when her daughter was growing up, though. A skilled editor, "she made me rewrite every English paper multiple times," Jane Ginsburg recalled. "That kind of paid off the other way round, when she would give me the drafts of her briefs, and I got to read them and make editing suggestions." A Harvard Law graduate, Jane Ginsburg is now a professor of literary and artistic property law at Columbia University. (Her brother, James, runs a classical music label in Chicago. Clara Spera, another Harvard Law alumna, is a federal law clerk in New York.)

To anyone who was around the Ginsburgs, their unusual parity was obvious. But to financiers and development executives, the character of Martin Ginsburg as a supportive husband was far-fetched. Backers offered to fund the film if he was rewritten as angrier, or less understanding; maybe he should threaten to divorce his wife, if she didn't drop the case.

"It came up *a lot*," Stiepleman said. "I remember at some point saying in a meeting, There's a 5,000-year history of narrative, of men coming home from battle, and their wives patch them up and boost their egos and send them back out to fight again. You write *one* supportive husband, and everyone's like, such a creature could never exist!"

For Hammer, the chance to play second fiddle was rare, and welcome. "I'm sure that women feel like they've been stuck in these supportive roles for a long time, but for me, to get to play something like this was amazing, because it's fair," he said. "And I think that there is a lot to be gained from seeing that a man can be an even better and stronger man, while still being an incredibly supportive husband and a buttress for his wife. It didn't make him any less of a man. If anything, it made him more."

Representing that dynamic may be one reason Justice Ginsburg gave the film her greenlight. "My mother strongly believes there won't be true equality until men take full participation in child care and other household tasks," her daughter said. The justice's chambers are decorated with photos of her son-in-law gazing at his infant son, and now her grandson gazing at her great-granddaughter.

She also wanted the practice of law to be depicted accurately. It was a reverence Stiepleman couldn't miss: for Hanukkah, "every year from the ages of 5 to 12, she gave me a copy of the U.S. Constitution," he said. (As a child he was mystified by the gift; as a teenager, inspired. Only as an adult did he realize the likely truth: "I was like, oh, of course, she has a discount at the Supreme Court gift shop. And she's reeeally busy.")

Her other big note, he said, was that she didn't want moviegoers to think that she alone shattered legal barriers, "as if it had never occurred to anyone else that women should be considered equal."

"She said, 'I built my career on the shoulders of women who came before me, like Dorothy Kenyon, like Pauli Murray, and people should know that,'" Stiepleman added. He wrote Kenyon, the pioneering feminist social activist and lawyer, into the script.

The original story ended differently, but (spoiler alert) Leder wanted to close on an image of the real Justice Ginsburg. Her cameo was set for the last day of filming; the justice picked her own costume, a sapphire-blue coat and dress, which she kept afterward. Starting on the steps of the Supreme Court, they did two takes, and then, Leder recalled, she asked the justice if she could do another. The reply, in a stern voice: "Just one more."

The moment, as an 85-year-old woman ascends into her future, brings audiences to tears.

Justice Ginsburg was not immune. At a friends-and-family showing, she and Claire Stiepleman, her sister-in-law, held hands from the moment their Marty appeared onscreen, her nephew said.

"I always thought she was just doing me a favor," letting me tell her story, he added. "But then right after she saw the movie, she gave me a hug and she said, 'Thank you.' And it never occurred to me, until that moment, that it was something we had done for each other."

Glossary

advocate Someone who supports an idea or cause.

affirmative action The practice of favoring individuals, usually in education or employment, who belong to a group that has been or continues to be discriminated against.

aptitude The skill to do something.

bipartisanship Cooperation between typically opposing political parties that want to find a compromise.

clerk Someone who assists a judge with legal research and other tasks.

collegiality A cooperative and equal relationship between co-workers.

conservatism A political philosophy favoring traditional social and cultural values.

discrimination Unfair treatment toward a group of people based on a characteristic or identifying factor such as gender or race.

ebullient Joyful, energetic and upbeat.

exempt Dismissed or excused from an obligation.

generalization A broad assumption or statement about a group based on little evidence.

judicial Relating to a legal judgment or the specific judge themselves.

jurisprudence The study and idea of law.

legislature An elected group of politicians in a state or country who can make or change laws for their citizens.

liberalism A political philosophy favoring a range of more modern ideas of liberty and equality.

litigation The course of taking legal action.

nomination The act of appointing or proposing someone for appointment to an office.

overturn To reverse a prior decision.

parley A conference that is held to discuss important issues.

partisan Dedicated to one political party or cause and refusing to compromise.

paucity A very small amount.

polemical Being very outspoken and controversial.

provision A statement in a legal document that requires a certain action must be satisfied before something else can happen.

swing vote An unpredictable group or person who has the power to decide the result of an election.

unanimous When all members of a group agree on the same decision.

U.S. Supreme Court justice An appointed court official who, along with the other justices, holds the power to vote on some of the most important landmark cases in the Supreme Court. This is a lifelong position, barring circumstances such as retirement or death.

welfare Government support that provides people with basic human necessities like food and shelter.

Media Literacy Terms

"Media literacy" refers to the ability to access, understand, critically assess and create media. The following terms are important components of media literacy, and they will help you critically engage with the articles in this title.

angle The aspect of a news story on which a journalist focuses and develops.

attribution The method by which a source is identified or by which facts and information are assigned to the person who provided them.

balance Principle of journalism that both perspectives of an argument should be presented in a fair way.

chronological order Method of writing a story presenting the details of the story in the order in which they occurred.

commentary Type of story that is an expression of opinion on recent events by a journalist generally known as a commentator.

credibility The quality of being trustworthy and believable, said of a journalistic source.

critical review Type of story that describes an event or work of art, such as a theater performance, film, concert, book, restaurant, radio or television program, exhibition or musical piece, and offers critical assessment of its quality and reception.

editorial Article of opinion or interpretation.

feature story Article designed to entertain as well as to inform.

headline Type, usually 18 point or larger, used to introduce a story.

human interest story Type of story that focuses on individuals and how events or issues affect their lives, generally offering a sense of relatability to the reader.

impartiality Principle of journalism that a story should not reflect a journalist's bias and should contain balance.

intention The motive or reason behind something, such as the publication of a news story.

interview story Type of story in which the facts are gathered primarily by interviewing another person or persons.

motive The reason behind something, such as the publication of a news story or a source's perspective on an issue.

news story An article or style of expository writing that reports news, generally in a straightforward fashion and without editorial comment.

op-ed An opinion piece that reflects a prominent individual's opinion on a topic of interest.

paraphrase The summary of an individual's words, with attribution, rather than a direct quotation of their exact words.

quotation The use of an individual's exact words indicated by the use of quotation marks and proper attribution.

reliability The quality of being dependable and accurate, said of a journalistic source.

rhetorical device Technique in writing intending to persuade the reader or communicate a message from a certain perspective.

source The origin of the information reported in journalism.

style A distinctive use of language in writing or speech; also a news or publishing organization's rules for consistent use of language with regard to spelling, punctuation, typography and capitalization, usually regimented by a house style guide.

tone A manner of expression in writing or speech.

Media Literacy Questions

1. Identify the various sources cited in the article "Law Parley Finds Women Lagging in Rights" (on page 20). How does Lesley Oelsner attribute information to each of these sources in the article? How effective are Oelsner's attributions in helping the reader identify her sources?

2. In "Kagan Says Her Path to Supreme Court Was Made Smoother by Ginsburg's" (on page 72), Adam Liptak directly quotes Elena Kagan. What are the strengths of the use of a direct quote as opposed to a paraphrase? What are the weaknesses?

3. Compare the headlines of "Rejected as a Clerk, Chosen as a Justice: Ruth Joan Bader Ginsburg" (on page 36) and "Supreme Court Upholds Workplace Arbitration Contracts Barring Class Actions" (on page 117). Which is a more compelling headline, and why? How could the less compelling headline be changed to better draw the reader's interest?

4. What type of story is "Justice Ginsburg's Cautious Radicalism" (on page 133)? Can you identify another article in this collection that is the same type of story? What elements helped you come to your conclusion?

5. Does Adam Liptak demonstrate the journalistic principle of impartiality in his article "On Justice Ginsburg's Summer Docket: Blunt Talk on Big Cases" (on page 75)? If so, how did he do so? If not, what could he have included to make his article more impartial?

6. The article "The Unsinkable R.B.G." (on page 128) is an example of an op-ed. Identify how Gail Collins's attitude and tone help convey her opinion on the topic.

7. Does "Bringing to Life the Ruth Bader Ginsburg Only Her Family Knows" (on page 205) use multiple sources? What are the strengths of using multiple sources in a journalistic piece? What are the weaknesses of relying heavily on only one or a few sources?

8. "In Her First Case, Ginsburg Dissents" (on page 82) features a photograph. What does this photograph add to the article?

9. " 'Notorious RBG: The Life and Times of Ruth Bader Ginsburg' " (on page 185) is an example of a critical review. What is the purpose of a critical review? Do you feel this article achieved that purpose?

10. What is the intention of the article "Ginsburg Leaves Hospital; Prognosis on Cancer Is Good" (on page 163)? How effectively does it achieve its intended purpose?

11. Analyze the authors' reporting in "Military College Can't Bar Women, High Court Rules" (on page 85) and "Ninja Supreme Court Justice: Ruth Bader Ginsburg Has Fun With Fame" (on page 196). Do you think one journalist is more balanced in her reporting than the other? If so, why do you think so?

12. "Ruth Bader Ginsburg and Gloria Steinem on the Unending Fight for Women's Rights" (on page 138) is an example of an interview. Can you identify skills or techniques used by Philip Galanes to gather information from Ruth Bader Ginsburg and Gloria Steinem?

Citations

All citations in this list are formatted according to the Modern Language Association's (MLA) style guide.

BOOK CITATION

THE NEW YORK TIMES EDITORIAL STAFF. *Ruth Bader Ginsburg*. New York: New York Times Educational Publishing, 2020.

ONLINE ARTICLE CITATIONS

CARMON, IRIN. "Justice Ginsburg's Cautious Radicalism." *The New York Times*, 24 Oct. 2015, www.nytimes.com/2015/10/25/opinion/sunday/justice-ginsburgs-cautious-radicalism.html.

CHOKSHI, NIRAJ. "Ruth Bader Ginsburg Is Discharged From Hospital After Surgery." *The New York Times*, 26 Dec. 2018, www.nytimes.com/2018/12/26/us/ruth-bader-ginsburg-hospital-cancer.html.

COLLINS, GAIL. "The Unsinkable R.B.G." *The New York Times*, 20 Feb. 2015, www.nytimes.com/2015/02/22/opinion/sunday/gail-collins-ruth-bader-ginsburg-has-no-interest-in-retiring.html.

DONADIO, RACHEL. "Justice Ruth Bader Ginsburg Presides Over Shylock's Appeal." *The New York Times*, 26 July 2016, www.nytimes.com/2016/07/28/theater/ruth-bader-ginsburg-rbg-venice-merchant-of-venice.html.

GALANES, PHILIP. "Ruth Bader Ginsburg and Gloria Steinem on the Unending Fight for Women's Rights." *The New York Times*, 14 Nov. 2015, www.nytimes.com/2015/11/15/fashion/ruth-bader-ginsburg-and-gloria-steinem-on-the-unending-fight-for-womens-rights.html.

GREENHOUSE, LINDA. "Bush Prevails; By Single Vote, Justices End Recount, Blocking Gore After 5-Week Struggle." *The New York Times*, 13 Dec. 2000, www.nytimes.com/2000/12/13/us/bush-prevails-single-vote-justices-end-recount-blocking-gore-after-5-week.html.

GREENHOUSE, LINDA. "From Top Law School Grad to Notorious R.B.G.: The

Evolution of a Supreme Court Justice." *The New York Times*, 29 Oct. 2018, www.nytimes.com/2018/10/29/books/review/ruth-bader-ginsburg -biography-jane-sherron-de-hart.html.

GREENHOUSE, LINDA. "Ginsburg at Fore in Court's Give-and-Take." *The New York Times*, 14 Oct. 1993, www.timesmachine.nytimes.com /timesmachine/1993/10/14/105593.html.

GREENHOUSE, LINDA. "In Her First Case, Ginsburg Dissents." *The New York Times*, 2 Sept. 1993, www.timesmachine.nytimes.com /timesmachine/1993/09/02/455093.html.

GREENHOUSE, LINDA. "Justice Ginsburg and the Price of Equality." *The New York Times*, 22 June 2017, www.nytimes.com/2017/06/22/opinion/ruth -bader-ginsburg-supreme-court.html.

GREENHOUSE, LINDA. "Justices' Ruling Limits Suits on Pay Disparity." *The New York Times*, 30 May 2007, www.nytimes.com/2007/05/30/washington /30scotus.html.

GREENHOUSE, LINDA. "Military College Can't Bar Women, High Court Rules." *The New York Times*, 27 June 1996, www.nytimes.com/1996/06/27/us /supreme-court-discrimination-military-college-can-t-bar-women-high -court-rules.html.

GREENHOUSE, LINDA. "On Privacy and Equality; Judge Ginsburg Still Voices Strong Doubts on Rationale Behind Roe v. Wade Ruling." *The New York Times*, 16 June 1993, www.timesmachine.nytimes.com/timesmachine /1993/06/16/943093.html.

GREENHOUSE, LINDA. "Oral Dissents Give Ginsburg a New Voice on Court." *The New York Times*, 31 May 2007, www.nytimes.com/2007/05/31 /washington/31scotus.html.

GREENHOUSE, LINDA. "Ruth Ginsburg Has Surgery for Cancer." *The New York Times*, 18 Sept. 1999, www.nytimes.com/1999/09/18/us/ruth -ginsburg-has-surgery-for-cancer.html.

GREENHOUSE, LINDA. "Senate, 96-3, Easily Affirms Judge Ginsburg as a Justice." *The New York Times*, 4 Aug. 1993, www.timesmachine.nytimes .com/timesmachine/1993/08/04/569993.html.

GREENHOUSE, LINDA. " 'Sisters in Law' Looks at Sandra Day O'Connor and Ruth Bader Ginsburg." *The New York Times*, 14 Sept. 2015, www.nytimes .com/2015/09/20/books/review/sisters-in-law-looks-at-sandra-day -oconnor-and-ruth-bader-ginsburg.html.

GREENHOUSE, STEVEN. "Supreme Court Raises Bar to Prove Job Discrimina-

tion." *The New York Times*, 24 June 2013, www.nytimes.com/2013/06/25
/business/supreme-court-raises-bar-to-prove-job-discrimination.html.

JOHNSTON, RICHARD J. H. "A Widower Sues for Benefits." *The New York
Times*, 11 Mar. 1973, www.timesmachine.nytimes.com/timesmachine
/1973/03/11/90923517.html.

KORNBLUT, ANNE E. "Justice Ginsburg Backs Value of Foreign Law." *The New
York Times*, 2 Apr. 2005, www.nytimes.com/2005/04/02/politics/justice
-ginsburg-backs-value-of-foreign-law.html.

LABATON, STEPHEN. "The Man Behind the High Court Nominee." *The New
York Times*, 17 June 1993, www.timesmachine.nytimes.com/timesmachine
/1993/06/17/598793.html.

LEWIS, NEIL A. "Ginsburg Promises Judicial Restraint if She Joins Court."
The New York Times, 21 July 1993, www.timesmachine.nytimes.com
/timesmachine/1993/07/21/991493.html.

LEWIS, NEIL A. "Rejected as a Clerk, Chosen as a Justice: Ruth Joan Bader
Ginsburg." *The New York Times*, 15 June 1993, www.timesmachine.nytimes
.com/timesmachine/1993/06/15/764493.html.

LIPTAK, ADAM. "Court Is 'One of Most Activist,' Ginsburg Says, Vowing to
Stay." *The New York Times*, 24 Aug. 2013, www.nytimes.com/2013/08/25
/us/court-is-one-of-most-activist-ginsburg-says-vowing-to-stay.html.

LIPTAK, ADAM. "Ginsburg Has Surgery for Pancreatic Cancer." *The New York
Times*, 5 Feb. 2009, www.nytimes.com/2009/02/06/washington/06ginsburg
.html.

LIPTAK, ADAM. "Justice Ruth Bader Ginsburg Misses Supreme Court Arguments." *The New York Times*, 7 Jan. 2019, www.nytimes.com/2019/01/07
/us/politics/justice-ginsburg-miss-supreme-court.html.

LIPTAK, ADAM. "Kagan Says Her Path to Supreme Court Was Made Smoother
by Ginsburg's." *The New York Times*, 10 Feb. 2014, www.nytimes.com/2014
/02/11/us/kagan-says-her-path-to-supreme-court-was-made-smoother-by
-ginsburg.html.

LIPTAK, ADAM. "On Justice Ginsburg's Summer Docket: Blunt Talk on Big
Cases." *The New York Times*, 31 July 2017, www.nytimes.com/2017/07/31
/us/politics/ruth-bader-ginsburg.html.

LIPTAK, ADAM. "On Tour With Notorious R.B.G., Judicial Rock Star." *The
New York Times*, 8 Feb. 2018, www.nytimes.com/2018/02/08/us/politics
/ruth-bader-ginsburg.html.

LIPTAK, ADAM. "Ruth Bader Ginsburg Is Cancer Free After Surgery, Supreme

Court Says." *The New York Times*, 11 Jan. 2019, www.nytimes.com/2019/01
/11/us/politics/ruth-bader-ginsburg-health-cancer-surgery.html.

LIPTAK, ADAM. "Ruth Bader Ginsburg, No Fan of Donald Trump, Critiques
Latest Term." *The New York Times*, 10 July 2016, www.nytimes.com/2016
/07/11/us/politics/ruth-bader-ginsburg-no-fan-of-donald-trump-critiques
-latest-term.html.

LIPTAK, ADAM. "Ruth Bader Ginsburg Regrets Speaking Out on Colin Kaepernick." *The New York Times*, 14 Oct. 2016, www.nytimes.com/2016/10/15
/us/ruth-bader-ginsburg-colin-kaepernick-national-anthem.html.

LIPTAK, ADAM. "Ruth Bader Ginsburg Undergoes Cancer Surgery." *The
New York Times*, 21 Dec. 2018, www.nytimes.com/2018/12/21/us/politics
/ruth-bader-ginsburg-cancer.html.

LIPTAK, ADAM. "Supreme Court Bars Favoring Mothers Over Fathers in Citizenship Case." *The New York Times*, 12 June 2017, www.nytimes.com/2017/06
/12/us/politics/supreme-court-citizenship-ginsburg-gorsuch.html.

LIPTAK, ADAM. "Supreme Court Upholds Workplace Arbitration Contracts
Barring Class Actions." *The New York Times*, 21 May 2018, www.nytimes
.com/2018/05/21/business/supreme-court-upholds-workplace-arbitration
-contracts.html.

MARGOLICK, DAVID. "Day Cites Law Role of Women." *The New York Times*,
14 Apr. 1984, www.timesmachine.nytimes.com/timesmachine/1984
/04/14/123081.html.

THE NEW YORK TIMES. "Columbia Professor Studied for Federal Court Post."
The New York Times, 16 Dec. 1979, www.timesmachine.nytimes.com
/timesmachine/1979/12/16/111209219.html.

THE NEW YORK TIMES. "In Her Own Words: Ruth Bader Ginsburg." *The New
York Times*, 15 June 1993, www.timesmachine.nytimes.com/timesmachine
/1993/06/15/810193.html.

THE NEW YORK TIMES. "The Legal Profession Is Absorbing an Influx of
Women." *The New York Times*, 18 Apr. 1978, www.timesmachine.nytimes
.com/timesmachine/1978/04/18/110836627.html.

THE NEW YORK TIMES. "Transcript of President's Announcement and Judge
Ginsburg's Remarks." *The New York Times*, 15 June 1993, www
.timesmachine.nytimes.com/timesmachine/1993/06/15/859493.html.

OELSNER, LESLEY. "Columbia Law Snares a Prize in the Quest for Women
Professors." *The New York Times*, 26 Jan. 1972, www.timesmachine
.nytimes.com/timesmachine/1972/01/26/81892659.html.

OELSNER, LESLEY. "Law Parley Finds Women Lagging in Rights." *The New York Times*, 27 Mar. 1975, www.timesmachine.nytimes.com/timesmachine /1975/03/27/76341092.html.

OELSNER, LESLEY. "3-Piece Suits, Not Women, Scarce at a Law Parley." *The New York Times*, 23 Mar. 1975, www.nytimes.com/1975/03/23 /archives/3piece-suits-not-women-scarce-at-a-law-parley.html.

ROBBINS, LIZ. "Justice Ginsburg Urges New Citizens to Make America Better." *The New York Times*, 10 Apr. 2018, www.nytimes.com/2018/04/10/nyregion /supreme-court-ruth-bader-ginsburg-naturalization-ceremony.html.

RYZIK, MELENA. "Bringing to Life the Ruth Bader Ginsburg Only Her Family Knows." *The New York Times*, 27 Dec. 2018, www.nytimes.com/2018/12/27 /movies/on-the-basis-of-sex-ruth-bader-ginsburg.html.

RYZIK, MELENA. "Ninja Supreme Court Justice: Ruth Bader Ginsburg Has Fun With Fame." *The New York Times*, 9 May 2018, www.nytimes .com/2018/05/09/movies/ruth-bader-ginsburg-rbg-documentary.html.

SCOTT, A.O. "In 'RBG,' the Life and Times of a Beloved and Controversial Supreme Court Justice." *The New York Times*, 3 May 2018, www.nytimes .com/2018/05/03/movies/rbg-review-documentary.html.

SENIOR, JENNIFER. " 'Notorious RBG: The Life and Times of Ruth Bader Ginsburg.' " *The New York Times*, 25 Oct. 2015, www.nytimes.com/2015 /10/26/books/review-notorious-rbg-the-life-and-times-of-ruth-bader -ginsburg.html.

STOLBERG, SHERYL GAY. "Ginsburg Leaves Hospital; Prognosis on Cancer Is Good." *The New York Times*, 29 Sept. 1999, www.nytimes.com/1999/09/29 /us/ginsburg-leaves-hospital-prognosis-on-cancer-is-good.html.

SULLIVAN, EILEEN. "Justice Ruth Bader Ginsburg Hospitalized With 3 Broken Ribs." *The New York Times*, 8 Nov. 2018, www.nytimes.com/2018/11/08/us /politics/ruth-bader-ginsburg-hospitalized.html.

TAYLOR, STUART, JR. "Court Rejects an F.C.C. Curb on 'Indecency' in Broadcasts." *The New York Times*, 30 July 1988, www.timesmachine.nytimes.com /timesmachine/1988/07/30/020888.html.

Index

This book is current up until the time of printing. For the most up-to-date reporting, visit www.nytimes.com.